First edition
Copyright © 2009 Alastair Sawday Publishing Co. Ltd
Published in October 2009

Alastair Sawday Publishing Co. Ltd,
The Old Farmyard, Yanley Lane,
Long Ashton, Bristol BS41 9LR, UK
Tel: +44 (0)1275 395430
Web: www.sawdays.co.uk

Maps Maidenhead Cartographic Services
Printing Butler, Tanner & Dennis, Frome, UK
Front Cover photograph Nigel Temple/Garden Picture
Library/photolibrary.uk.com
Back Cover photographs 1. Loupe Images/Christopher Drake
2. Patrick Hilyer: La Colombière p52
3. Château du Tertre p124
Cover design Walker Jansseune

Series editor Alastair Sawday
Editor Patrick Hilyer
Editorial director Annie Shillito
Managing editor Jackie King
Accounts Bridget Bishop,
Amy Lancastle
Editorial Jo Boissevain, Angharad Barnes
Production Jules Richardson,
Rachel Coe, Tom Germain
Sales & Marketing & PR Rob Richardson,
Sarah Bolton, Bethan Riach, Lisa Walklin
Web & IT Chris Banks, Phil Clarke,
Mike Peake, Russell Wilkinson

ISBN-13: 978-1-906136-26-0

List of symbols

  At least one bedroom & bathroom accessible for wheelchair users. Phone for details.

  At least one bedroom and bathroom accessible without steps.

  No smoking anywhere in the property.

  Within 10 miles of a bus/coach/train station and owner can arrange collection.

  Good vegetarian dinner options (arrange in advance).

  Guests' pets can sleep in the bedroom (not on the bed).

  Owners' pets live on the property.

  Some, if not all, bedrooms are air-conditioned.

  Swimming pool on the premises; use may be by arrangement.

  Tennis court on the premises; use may be by arrangement.

  Bikes on the premises to hire or borrow.

  Children of all ages are welcome. Cots, highchairs, etc, are not necessarily available.

  Your host/booking contact speaks English, whether perfectly or not.

  Wireless internet access available for guests.

  Working farm or vineyard.

French Vineyards

Patrick Hilyer

Special Places to Stay
Bed and breakfasts, châteaux and gîtes on wine-producing estates

CONTENTS

OUR OFFICE AND CULTURE

The buildings

Beautiful as they were, our old offices leaked heat, used electricity to heat water and rooms, flooded spaces with light to illuminate one person, and were not ours to alter.

So in 2005 we created our own eco-offices by converting some old barns to create a low-emissions building. We made the building energy-efficient through a variety of innovative and energy-saving building techniques, described below.

Insulation We went to great lengths to ensure that very little heat can escape, by laying thick insulating board under the roof and floor and adding further insulation underneath the roof and between the rafters. We then lined the whole of the inside of the building with plastic sheeting to ensure air-tightness.

Heating We installed a wood-pellet boiler from Austria, in order to be largely fossil-fuel free. The pellets are made from compressed sawdust, a waste product from timber mills that work only with sustainably managed forests. The heat is conveyed by water, throughout the building, via an under-floor system.

Water We installed a 6000-litre tank to collect rainwater from the roofs. This is pumped back, via an ultra-violet filter, to the lavatories, showers and basins. There are two solar thermal panels on the roof providing heat to the one (massively insulated) hot-water cylinder.

Lighting We have a carefully planned mix of low-energy lighting: task lighting and up-lighting. We also installed sun-pipes to reflect the outside light into the building.

Electricity All our electricity has long come from the Good Energy company and is 100% renewable.

Materials Virtually all materials are non-toxic or natural. Our carpets are made from (80%) Herdwick sheep-wool from National Trust farms in the Lake District.

Doors and windows Outside doors and new windows are wooden, double-glazed and beautifully constructed in Norway. Old windows have been double-glazed.

We have a building we are proud of, and architects and designers are fascinated by. But best of all, we are now in a better position to encourage our owners and readers to take sustainability more seriously.

What we do

Besides having moved the business to a low-carbon building, the company works in a number of ways to reduce its overall environmental footprint.

Our footprint We measure our footprint annually and use it to find ways of reducing our environmental impact. To help address unavoidable carbon emissions we try to put something back: since 2006 we have supported SCAD, an organisation that works with villagers in India to create sustainable development.

Travel Staff are encouraged to car-share or cycle to work and we provide showers (rainwater-fed) and bike sheds. Our company cars run on LPG (liquid petroleum gas) or recycled cooking oil. We avoid flying and take the train for business trips wherever possible. All office travel is logged as part of our footprint and we count our freelance editors' and inspectors' miles too.

Our office Nearly all of our office waste is recycled; kitchen waste is composted and used in the office vegetable garden. Organic and fairtrade basic provisions are used in the staff kitchen and at in-house events, and green cleaning products are used throughout the office.

Working with owners We are proud that many of our Special Places help support their local economy and, through our Ethical Collection, we recognise owners who go the extra mile to serve locally sourced and organic food or those who have a positive impact on their environment or community.

Engaging readers We hope to raise awareness of the need for individuals to play their part; our Go Slow series places an emphasis on ethical travel and the Fragile Earth imprint consists of hard-hitting environmental titles. Our Ethical Collection informs readers about owners' ethical endeavours.

Ethical printing We print our books locally to support the British printing industry and to reduce our carbon footprint. We print our books on either FSC-certified or recycled paper, using vegetable or soy-based inks.

Our supply chain Our electricity is 100% renewable (supplied by Good Energy), and we put our savings with Triodos, a bank whose motives we trust. Most supplies are bought in bulk from a local ethical-trading co-operative.

A WORD FROM ALASTAIR SAWDAY

An old wine enthusiast, badly smashed in a railway accident, was given a drop of wine to revive him. 'Pauillac, 1899' he murmured, and then died.

It is a good story, but don't be daunted by the hint of connoisseurship. Let it not put you off making your own journey into the wonderful world of vineyards, winemaking and 'viticulteurs'. And do let me tell you why I think this book is such a startlingly good find.

High walls, elusive views, hints of beauty beyond sight, hidden places – such are the frustrations of the thwarted traveller. We have all known the curiosity aroused by a dense curtain of foliage hiding things we can only guess at. As we mosey through a village, admiring the church, the market square, the old fountain and the row of ancient shops, we often find ourselves unable to admire whatever it is that lies beyond the great gate at the edge of the village. This is especially so in France, where many villages and towns have at their edges a mighty, or even a mini, château standing guard protectively over its precious hectares of vineyard. You can only get a tantalising hint of what is there.

This remarkable book now swings open those gates, takes you up the tree-lined drive and right into the house! You are greeted at the door by the owners, swept inside, often with a glass of wine, and then shown your room – overlooking those vineyards and the village that is now on the other side of the gates. After dinner with the family, struggling with your French or slipping with relief back into your English, you sleep the sleep of the exuberant wine taster. The day brings the unfolding beauty of the estate, a tour around the cellars and winery and conversations about winemaking with your hosts. At harvest time you will perhaps join in, bent over the vines in one of Europe's most ancient rituals. You will certainly never be made to feel inadequate for knowing little and will be celebrated for offering to help.

We cover all the main wine regions, with old producers and new jostling together on these pages. Most of them are French, with the foreign growers coming from all over the place. The average estate size here is ten to fifteen hectares. Some are tiny, producing wine as impressive as the brave determination of the winemaker. Others produce wine that is ordinary, perhaps, but fascinating for the journey it has taken and the people who laboured to produce it. Some of the wines here are fine by any standards. What is perhaps most exciting about them all is that they are produced with deep commitment and sensitivity to the soil and the 'terroir'. There are no crazed exploiters of chemistry here, nobody wrenching the best out of the soil and vine without a thought for their future. These are the sort of people who have made France's wines famous throughout the world for their complexity and distinctiveness of place. They are as honest and devoted as the greatest of the wine-makers. (It is heartening to report that in many cases the children are returning to take over, especially where families are long-established.)

Some of these growers use the 'biodynamic' system. They are a special breed, unwavering in their commitment to a method that to the rest of us seems bizarre. It involves a fine sensitivity to the way that nature works. There is no space to explain it here, so read within or look it up on the web; it is a fascinating subject.

Led by biodynamic and organic producers, the rest of them have taken much of the central message to heart. France has it own way of compromising with the highest standards: 'agriculture raisonnée'. This is a commitment to using as few chemicals as possible, respecting the soil and its complexity, allowing natural growth (often just grass) between the vines.

So they are a richly interesting bunch. Among them are balloonists, teachers, chefs, artists, an Irish grower, and several English ones. They are fiercely independent, nearly all of them natural protagonists of the Slow movement. It is to Patrick's great credit that the variety of people and wines is so rich and rewarding. This book is his idea and so is most of the mighty labour behind it.

I end on a happy note: you can buy your wines on the spot at prices far lower than you would pay for them in Britain – if, indeed, they are available here. You are unlikely to get a special discount, but you will get good wines, massive generosity, kindness and knowledge. They are an irresistible combination.

Alastair Sawday

INTRODUCTION

We have brought together a huge variety of places to stay in this guide – some hosts offer you bed and breakfast, others have a gîte or a little apartment for you and others have all the bells and whistles of a smart hotel. Some have luxurious suites, others rustic little hideaways with red-checked kitchens. Almost the only thing they have in common is that they are all on wine-producing estates.

A good chunk of these owners, of course, have ecology at the top of their agenda and were 'green' before the expression was even thought of, such is their respect for nature and soil. Many have watched their ancestors nurture vines and tend food crops while using their knowledge of natural forces to get the best out of their land. Long may they continue to follow the slower path through life.

We are very keen in the write ups to draw attention to the owners green credentials and to mention the things they are doing to minimise their impact on their environment. But don't forget that you can play your part, too. Consider travelling by train to, and in, France; French trains are fast, efficient and cheap and, with a London–Paris journey time of just over two hours, you could be leaving St Pancras in the morning and be on a terrace overlooking a Loire vineyard by lunchtime, or on a warm Provençal rooftop for an early evening aperitif. Some owners will pick you up from the nearest train station and then lend bikes for local exploration.

HOW WE CHOOSE OUR PLACES

It's simple. There are no rules, no boxes to tick. We choose places that we like and are fiercely subjective in our choices. We also recognise that one person's idea of special is not necessarily someone else's so there is a variety of places, and prices, in the book. Those who are familiar with our guidebooks know that we look for comfort, originality, authenticity, and reject the insincere, the anonymous and the banal. The way guests are treated comes as high on our list as the setting, the architecture, the atmosphere and the food.

As well as running an unmistakably special place to stay, the owners in this guide also have to be producing wine of note and to be geared up to welcome those who want to learn more about their way of life, the wine they produce and the rhythms of rural life.

Inspections

We visit every place in the guide to get a feel for how both house and owner tick. We don't take a clipboard and we don't have a list of what is acceptable and what is not. Instead, we chat for an hour or so with the owner and look round. It's all very informal, but it gives us an excellent idea of who would enjoy staying there. If the visit happens to be the last of the day, we sometimes stay the night.

Feedback

In between inspections we rely on feedback from our army of readers, as well as from staff members who are encouraged to visit properties across the series. This feedback is invaluable to us and we always follow up on comments. So do tell us

whether your stay has been a joy or not, if the atmosphere was great or stuffy, the owners cheery or bored. The accuracy of the book depends on what you, and our inspectors, tell us.

A lot of the new entries in our guides are recommended by readers, so keep telling us about new places you've discovered and that you think would be a good addition to our series. Please use the forms on our website at www.sawdays.co.uk.

However, please do not tell us if the bedside light wasn't working, or the shower head broken. Tell the owner immediately, for most are more than happy to correct problems and will bend over backwards to help. Far better than bottling it up and then writing to us a week later!

Subscriptions

Owners pay to appear in this guide. Their fee goes towards the high costs of inspecting, of producing an all-colour book and of maintaining our website. We only include places that we like and find special for one reason or another, so it is not possible for anyone to buy their way onto these pages.

Disclaimer

We make no claims to pure objectivity in choosing these places. They are here simply because we like them. Our opinions and tastes are ours alone and this book is a statement of them; we hope you will share them. We have done our utmost to get our facts right but apologise unreservedly for any mistakes that may have crept in.

You should know that we don't check such things as fire regulations, swimming pool security or any other laws with which owners of properties receiving paying guests should comply. This is the responsibility of the owners.

USING THIS BOOK

Finding the right place for you

All of these places have been visited and then written about so that you can decide for yourself which will suit you. Those of you who swear by Sawday's books trust us precisely because we don't have a blanket standard; we include places simply because we like them. But we all have different priorities, so if something is particularly important to you then check when you book: a simple question or two can avoid misunderstandings.

If the entry mentions other gîtes and B&B, note that you may not be in total isolation but will most probably be sharing the pool and garden with other guests and their families. This shouldn't spoil your holiday but, if absolute peace is vital to you, ask the owners how many others are likely to be around.

Maps

Each property is flagged with its entry number on the maps at the front. These maps are a great starting point for planning your trip, but please don't use them as anything other than a general guide – use a decent road map for real navigation. Most places will send you detailed instructions once you have booked your stay.

Symbols

Below each entry you will see some symbols, which are explained at the very back of the book. They are based on the information given to us by the owners. However, things do change: bikes may be under repair or a new pool may have been put in. Please use the symbols as a guide rather than an absolute statement of fact and double-check anything that is important to you – owners occasionally bend their own rules, so it's worth asking if you may take your child or dog even if they don't have the symbol.

Children – The symbol shows places which are happy to accept children of all ages. This does not mean that they will necessarily have cots, high chairs, etc. Many who say no to children do so not because they don't like them but because they may have a steep stair, an unfenced pond or they find balancing the needs of mixed age groups too challenging.

Pets – Our symbol shows places which are happy to accept pets. It means they can sleep in the bedroom with you, but not on the bed. Be realistic about your pet – if it is nervous or excitable or doesn't like the company of other dogs, people, chickens, or children, then say so.

Owners' pets – The symbol is given when the owners have their own pet on the premises. It may not be a cat! But it is there to warn you that you may be greeted by a dog, serenaded by a parrot, or indeed sat upon by a cat.

PRACTICAL MATTERS

Types of places

Some places have rooms in annexes or stables, barns or garden 'wings', some of which feel part of the house, some of which don't. If you have a strong preference for being in the throng or for being apart, check those details. Consider your surroundings, too: rambling châteaux may be cooler than you are used to and working vineyards may occasionally be noisy. Some owners give you a front door key so you may come and go as you please; others like to have the house empty between, say, 10am and 4pm. Remember that B&Bs in this book are not hotels – don't expect room service, or your beds to be made, do go for a fascinating glimpse of a French way of life.

Rooms

Bedrooms – We tell you if a room is a double, twin/double (ie with zip and link beds), suite, family (any mix of beds for 3 or more people) or single. Owners can often juggle beds or bedrooms, so talk to them about what you need before you book. It is rare to be given your own room key in a B&B.

Bathrooms – Most bedrooms in this book have an en suite bath or shower room; we only mention bathroom details when they do not. So, you may get a 'separate' bathroom (yours alone but not in your room) or a shared bathroom. You may find a mention that two rooms share a bathroom and are 'let to same party only'. Please do not assume this means you must be a group of friends to apply; it simply means that if you book one of these rooms you will not be sharing a bathroom with strangers. For simplicity we generally refer to 'bath'. This

doesn't necessarily mean it has no shower; it could mean a shower only. If these things are important to you, please check when booking.

Sitting rooms – Most B&B owners offer guests the family sitting room to share, or they provide a sitting room specially for guests. If neither option is available we generally say so, but do check. And do not assume that every bedroom or sitting room has a TV.

When to go

Families with school-age children will generally take their main holiday in July and August, which is when the French will be taking theirs. For these months it is essential to book well in advance. If you can holiday outside those busy months, do so: it'll be slightly cooler, it'll be cheaper and you'll be less likely to get snarled up in traffic jams, especially on arrival and departure (avoid 15 August, the Assumption bank holiday, at all costs).

Out of season you also have a better chance of seeing France going about its everyday business. May and June are the best months for flowers, for temperatures suitable for walking, and for visiting the Mediterranean coast. If mushrooms are your thing, September's the time, and temperatures in autumn can be ideal. The winter months, when you often get clear fine days, are well worth considering too. Some holiday homes can be rented all year round, some close during the winter, others close during the winter but open for Christmas and New Year. Winter is often a good time to glimpse the real France; the weather in the south can be very pleasant and rates are normally

more reasonable. A word of warning, though: some restaurants in rural areas only open in July and August. Some markets too, but they tend to be the touristy and less authentic ones. Many restaurants close for the winter.

How many do the gîtes sleep?

In some instances, for self catering set ups, we give two figures, separated by a hyphen. The first figure is the number of adults the house sleeps comfortably; the second is the number of people who can actually fit in. Some owners can provide extra beds, though there may be an additional charge, and where sofabeds or mezzanine levels are provided, privacy may be compromised. If you want to bring extra people, you absolutely must ask the owner first. Some places offer special rates if you are fewer people than the number shown, though this generally applies out of season only.

In this book a 'double' means one double bed, a 'twin' means two single beds. A 'triple' is three single beds. 'Family rooms' include at least one double bed. Extra beds and cots for children, sometimes at extra cost, can often be provided – do ask. We don't give total numbers of bathrooms and shower rooms and nor do we give details about bathrooms being 'en suite' but many are, so check with the owners if this matters.

Facilities

If you choose to stay in one of the gîtes for a week it is probably important to you that it is properly equipped. If you can't manage without a microwave, dishwasher, TV, CD-player, barbecue or central heating, check with the owners first. Electric kettles are still a rarity in French-owned homes so if you can't manage without, bring your own. You may also want to consider bringing a portable fan as they can be a godsend in high summer. If you have your own electrical appliances bring an adaptor plug, as virtually all sockets are for two-pin plugs that run on 220/240 AC voltage.

Meals

Unless we say otherwise, breakfast is included at the chambres d'hôtes. This will usually be a good continental breakfast – traditionally pain de campagne with apricot jam and a bowl of coffee, but brioche, crêpes, croissants, and homemade cake are sometimes on offer too. Some owners are fairly unbending about breakfast times, others are happy to be flexible.

Apart from breakfast in B&Bs, no meals should be expected unless you have arranged them in advance. A few places here offer a table d'hôtes dinner to overnight guests. This means the same food for all and absolutely must be booked ahead, but will not be available every night. Meal prices are quoted per person, although children will usually eat for less. Ask your hosts about reduced meal rates if you're travelling with little ones. When wine is included this can mean a range of things, from a standard quarter-litre carafe per person to a barrel of table wine.

If you are staying on a self catering basis and dining out, be aware that rural restaurants stop taking orders at 9pm and often close at least one day a week.

Prices and minimum stays

Each B&B entry gives a price PER ROOM for two people. The price range covers a one-night stay in the cheapest room in low season to the most expensive in high season. Some owners charge more at certain times (during festivals, for example) and some charge less for stays of more than one night. Prices quoted are those given to us for 2009–2011 but are not guaranteed, so do double-check when booking. Gîte prices are usually for one week's rental.

Taxe de séjour is a small tax that local councils can levy on visitors; you may find your bill increased by €0.50–€2 per person per day to cover this.

Booking and cancellation

Do be clear about what you have booked and the price you will be charged. It is essential to book well ahead for July and August, and wise for other months. Owners may send you a booking form or contrat de location (tenancy contract) which must be filled in and returned, and commits both sides. Requests for deposits vary; some are non-refundable, and some owners may charge you for the whole of the booked stay in advance.

Some cancellation policies are more stringent than others. It is also worth noting that some owners will take this deposit directly from your credit/debit card without contacting you to discuss it. So ask them to explain their cancellation policy clearly before booking so you understand exactly where you stand; it may well avoid a nasty surprise.

Remember that the UK is one hour behind France and people can be upset by telephone enquiries coming through late in their evening.

Payment

If owners take credit cards we have given them the appropriate symbol. (Check that your particular credit card is acceptable.) Euro travellers' cheques will usually be accepted; other currency cheques are unpopular because of commission charges. Virtually all ATMs in France take Visa and MasterCard.

Tipping

Owners of the smaller places do not expect tips. If you have been treated with extraordinary kindness, write to them, or leave a small gift. Please tell us, too – we love to hear, and we do note, all feedback.

Arrivals and departures

Say roughly what time you will arrive (normally after 4pm for B&Bs), as most hosts like to welcome you personally. Be on time if you have booked dinner; if, despite best efforts, you are delayed, phone to give warning.

Closed

When given in months this means the whole of the month(s) stated. So, 'Closed: November–March' means closed from 1 November to 31 March.

After all the plotting and planning of your getaway, we hope you have a thoroughly wonderful time with these lovely people. On your return, don't forget to tell us about your stay, via our website.

Bon voyage!

KEY MAP
Wine regions

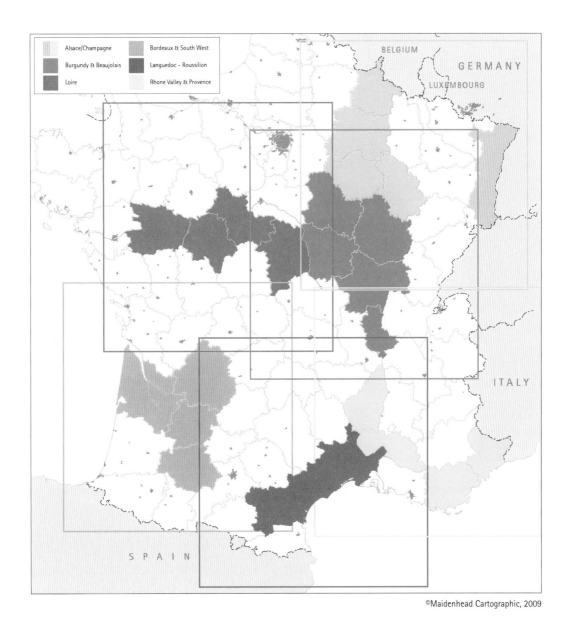

Legend:
- Alsace/Champagne
- Burgundy & Beaujolais
- Loire
- Bordeaux & South West
- Languedoc - Roussilion
- Rhone Valley & Provence

©Maidenhead Cartographic, 2009

ALSACE & CHAMPAGNE
Wine region

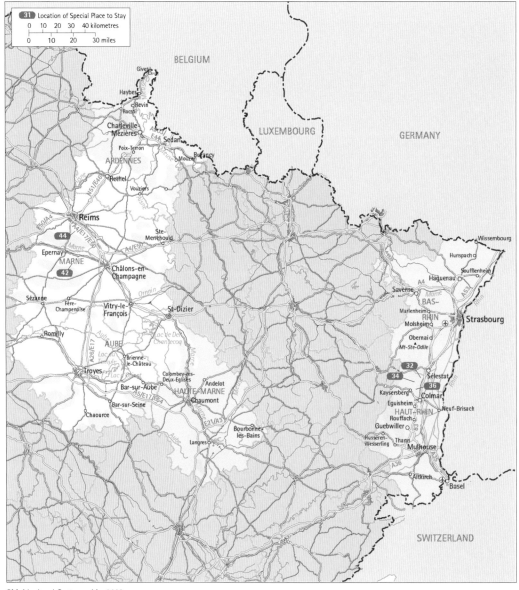

©Maidenhead Cartographic, 2009

BURGUNDY & BEAUJOLAIS
Wine region

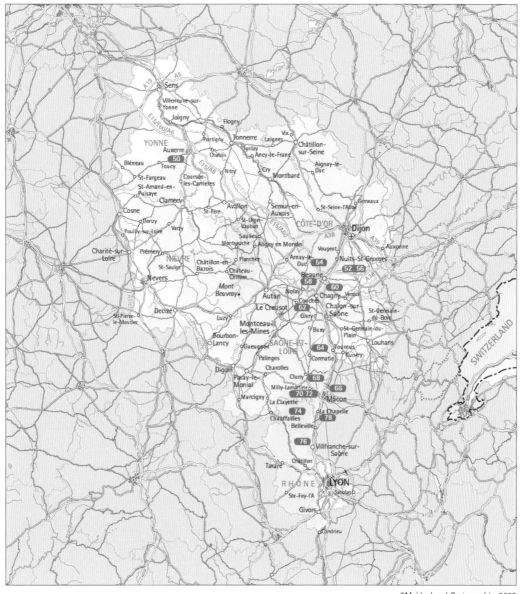

©Maidenhead Cartographic, 2009

LOIRE
Wine region

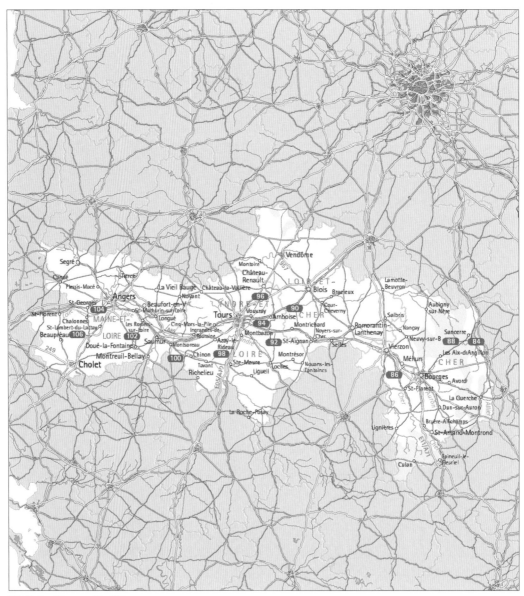

©Maidenhead Cartographic, 2009

BORDEAUX & SOUTH WEST
Wine region

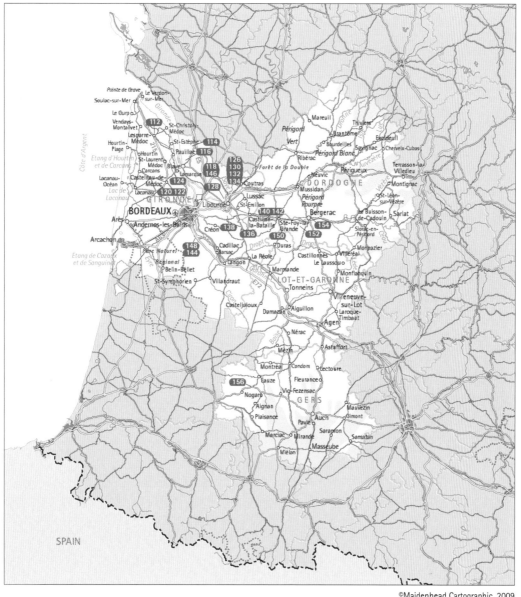

©Maidenhead Cartographic, 2009

LANGUEDOC – ROUSSILLON
Wine region

RHONE VALLEY & PROVENCE
Wine region

©Maidenhead Cartographic, 2009

ALSACE

ALSACE

Of all the French wine regions Alsace is one of the most distinctive and beautiful. Over its long history it has been claimed by both Germany – the local speech is a dialect of German – and France and, although now part of France, it has a strong, independent identity; the wines here too are very different from those in other regions.

The Alsace vineyards occupy a narrow north-to-south strip of land between the Vosges mountains and the Rhine valley. A complex geological history has given them a diverse range of terroirs and the underlying rock may be granite, red sandstone, fossil-rich limestone or marl. Above the rock is a varied subsoil, and this variety means that, as in Burgundy's vineyards, location is everything. Although the winters can be cold, the rift valley of the Rhine lies in the rain shadow of the Vosges, so summers are warm and dry – perfect weather for ripening grapes and for attracting tourists.

To understand the mainly dry, mostly white wines of Alsace you have to get to grips with grape variety. Floral, rich rieslings, raisiny muscats or spicy gewürztraminers – all the wines (apart from the sparkling crémants, and the everyday edelzwickers) specify one of seven grapes on the label. The best vineyards, planted with the so-called 'noble varietals', are classified as grand cru and there were 51 of them at the last count.

In favourable years the harvesting of the grand cru grapes can be delayed to allow them to shrivel and intensify their sugars, giving the 'vendages tardives' (late harvest) wines. When conditions allow, the picking can be further delayed to allow the fungus botrytis cinerea to develop, giving the highly-prized 'sélection de grains nobles'. Both give wines a luscious fruitiness, with the latter being the sweetest. They compare in many respects with Sauternes from Bordeaux, Coteaux du Layon from the Anjou and Germany's Trockenbeerenauslese, and are accordingly highly priced.

Eating out in Alsace is another reminder of the region's Teutonic past. Choucroute (the Alsatian variety of sauerkraut) was created here, and has spread all over France as a popular brasserie meal. Pork is popular, and is a central ingredient of 'baeckeoffe', a local potato hotpot that can include other meats and even snails. Freshwater fish is often cooked in riesling wine. Instead of the universal pizza you will find 'flammeküeche', or its vegetarian version 'zweibelküeche' (in French, tarte à l'oignon). Local desserts include the cake called 'kougelhopf', or tarte Alsacienne, a custard tart with plums.

The geography that contributes to the quality of Alsace's wine also creates its picturesque scenery. Wooded hilltops give way to terraces of vines that sometimes seem too steep to cultivate. Many of the towns and villages along the Route des Vins (which runs for over 100 miles) have a medieval charm, the ruined castles, fortified churches and walled towns testify to a violent past. Do visit Strasbourg, a beautiful city, with a lovely cathedral and an ancient university and Nancy with its impressive 18th-century centre, around the Place Stanislaus.

La Cour du Bailli

HAUT-RHIN

The fortifications encircling Bergheim recall the town's medieval might; its double line of defensive walls with their gateways and towers are better preserved than those in other villages along the Alsace wine route. The Halbeisen family, whose forbears include a knight of Emperor Frederick III, came here in 1737 and started a wine dynasty that has flourished for over 250 years. Their noble ancestor's coat of arms still appears on the Halbeisen wine label. Three generations live here: Émile, his daughter Yvette and grandson Aurélian – the most recent guardian. The winery is a short stroll from their splendid hotel and spa – La Cour du Bailli.

Horse-drawn wagons once trundled through the grand arched gateway. Now the courtyard of La Cour has prettily laid tables and colourful pots and baskets. Beneath the courtyard is a dining room in the stone vaults of an ancient wine cellar. A vine-festooned gallery leads to the delightful bedrooms where beautiful 18th-century painted interiors and furniture, dark panelled timber floors, and venerable oak beams have been carefully conserved. On the first floor overlooking the quad and in an adjoining farmhouse are thirty-eight studios and apartments, the largest of which have balconies or patios with views of Bergheim's pantiled roofs and forested hills. Below the farm, in a secret subterranean realm, are treatment rooms and a spa where you can bathe in a pool built inside an ancient barrel vault, relax in the sanarium ("not as hot as a sauna and less steamy than a hammam"), or try grape-based body treatments. From La Cour you cross the ramparts and the little Bergenbach river to reach the winery. Émile, now enjoying his retirement, often takes his evening apéro on the sunny patio in front of the house. Through a doorway, framed by a rambling vine, is

WINES

Domaine Halbeisen, Alsace Gewürztraminer Rotenberg
Late harvest ('vendanges tardives') grapes are carefully selected from the Rotenberg vineyard to make this deep and complex wine. The aromatic mix of flowers, spices and citrus gives you a different experience with each sniff. Its sweetness is balanced by a juicy acidity. Great with Asian cuisine like sweet and sour pork spare ribs, or southern Indian curries.
Wines €5–€20

Aurélien Halbeisen
La Cour du Bailli,
57 grand rue, 68750 Bergheim
- Rooms: 38 twins/doubles, €71–€185.
  2 gîtes for 4, €102–€115 per night.
- Meals: Buffet breakfast €10, book ahead.
  Half-board €28 p.p. extra.
- Closed: Never.
- +33 (0)3 89 73 73 46
- www.cour-bailli.com

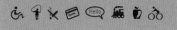

the tasting room – Christine will take you on a tour of the cellars, then bring you here to the long oak-topped counter. Seven grape varieties are cultivated on Bergheim's marl and limestone slopes. "Apart from the dry, medium-dry and sweet late harvest styles, there's a pinot noir for red wine stalwarts," says Christine. The riesling, from the south-facing grand cru vineyard of Altenberg just behind the winery, is sublime.

A little knowledge gained at the winery will prepare you for the restaurant's impressive wine list. Several of the wines are used to prepare rich, wholesome dishes like terrine au muscat or coq au riesling. The wines make it into the desserts, too – try the fruit pudding 'kougelhopf' served with Marc de Gewürztraminer ice cream!

Walk along the high city walls for a bird's eye view of the neat gardens cultivated between the backs of the houses and the ramparts; after, drop down into a shady square for coffee. Neuf-Brisach is another fortified town: designed 300 years ago by the famous architect Vauban, it is an unrivalled example of 18th-century defensive skill and is a world heritage site.

Domaine Agapé

HAUT-RHIN

'Agapé' is the Greek word for love. When Vincent and Isabelle bought this property in 2007 it seemed to them a perfect name for their new home and winemaking business as it conveyed their love of food and wine.

They each come from a family of winemakers and the combining of their talents has created a small family winery with a burgeoning reputation. For those on a tour of Alsace this is a perfect base, half way down the Alsace Route des Vins, which runs from Marlenheim in the north to Thann in the south. Vincent, an enthusiastic, intelligent communicator, offers tasting tours of his award-winning pinot blancs, rieslings and gewürtztraminers; Isabelle runs cookery classes in nearby Colmar, the town called 'little Venice'.

There are three compact and cosy apartments in a new cottage next door to the winery. Simply furnished, each double bedroom has a big neat kitchen, a small dining area and a spotless modern shower room. From the windows and the balcony that overlook the vines you can see both of Riquewihr's church spires. The medieval town in the foothills of the Vosges mountains sits in the centre of this, one of France's most beautiful wine regions. It is known as the 'Pearl of Alsace'. A few minutes walk or cycle ride (bikes are available) brings you to the village, whose fortified walls encircle a labyrinth of cobbled medieval streets and half-timbered houses. Glimpsed from the corner of every narrow alleyway are the vineyards. A quiet lane leads to the woods and the regional park of the Ballons des Vosges – 3,000 square kilometers of natural wilderness, forested peaks and ancient hidden castles.

Vincent inherited his wine lore from his family and you will find several wine-making Sipps in the area. His vines cover just over eight hectares (a third of which are classified as grand cru) and are divided into small parcels on the best limestone côtes at Riquewihr, Hunawihr and Ribauvillé. Vincent cultivates his vines using his own organic methods

like using homemade compost and organic insecticides but opposes official classification of 'biologique'. He prefers to focus on the quality of the grape instead; he harvests his crops by hand and slowly ferments before blending.

Three wine styles are produced: the aromatic and fruity Expression wines; the complex and mineral grands crus; and the late harvest Hélios wines. Made only in the sunniest years, these rich, honeyed and mouthwateringly juicy rieslings can last for decades.

Vincent has an encyclopaedic knowledge of the history and culture of his homeland. Apart from his native French, the Alsatian dialect, and German, he speaks such excellent English that it's surprising to learn he has never lived or worked in England. He will tell you where to find the best restaurants, fortified churches, châteaux, and astounding views. The unofficial symbol of Alsace is the stork but the birds had all but disappeared a few decades ago. Now, thanks to the efforts of ecologists, they are back and you'll see them roosting on specially constructed rooftop platforms in most villages.

WINES

Domaine Agapé,
Alsace Grand Cru Rosacker Riesling
Minty fresh with a hint of lime, the aromas prepare you for the explosion of lemon sherbet that follows and a mouthwateringly long lemony finish. Mineral, elegant and balanced, this fluted bottle of Alsace sunshine is perfect for the fish broth, Matelote du Rhin. Or try it with the famous Alsatian hotpot 'baekaoffa'.

Wines €7–€30

Isabelle & Vincent Sipp
Domaine Agapé,
10 rue des Tuileries, 68340 Riquewihr
- Rooms: 3 twins/doubles, €350.
  3 gîtes for 2-4, from €60 per night, from €350 per week.
- Meals: Restaurant 200m.
- Closed: Rarely.
- +33 (0)3 89 47 94 23
- www.alsace-agape.fr

Domaine Horcher

HAUT-RHIN

The villages along the Alsace wine route are a joy to discover. Linked by country lanes, snaking through the vine-covered hillsides, their churches, colourful half-timbered houses and narrow cobbled streets have altered little since the Middle Ages. Between the medieval towns of Colmar and Ribeauvillé is the little town of Mittelwihr. The toponym 'wihr' signifies a fortified settlement (there are many along the route) so Mittelwihr means 'middle town'.

On the road that leads to Riquewihr is the home of Alfred and Irène Horcher. A typical family of independent vignerons, three generations of Horchers live and work in the house and winery. Alfred's mother, now in her eighties, still helps out with the late spring palisage – the manual trellising of the vines – and the rose garden in front of the house shows off her green-fingered flair. The generous and genuinely welcoming Alfred

and Irène run the domaine with their two grown-up children. "We are always true to tradition and respectful of nature," says Alfred. They cultivate their vineyards using the very minimum of chemical treatments and only organic fertilisers.

The Horchers have two modern and convivial gîtes next to the winery. Beside a wooded stream Les Merles is a charming two-storey, timber-framed gîte with room for a family of five. On the first floor is a compact contemporary kitchen and a wonderfully light open-plan dining/living area with two balconies, one overlooking the courtyard, the other, the stream. Two bedrooms are reached via a central open staircase; the bright double has a round portal looking out onto the woods behind; for children there's a triple room with bunks.

Le Vignoble is a smart contemporary apartment above one of the winery buildings. Reached from an external steel stairway, the rooms

have big windows and balconies looking out over the vineyards. Both gîtes have private outdoor eating areas.

Irène shares Alfred's passion for the region's produce. She serves the wines of the domaine in a delightful tasting room next to the cellars. "We grow seven different cepages," Irene explains, "for our dry, medium-dry, sweet and sparkling wines." Starting with a glass of creamy-fizzy Crémant (a worthy alternative to Champagne) she explains: "The grape variety is king and the choice of where to grow each one depends on the soil. So, muscat vines that are suited to one area are not grown in another that might be better for sylvaner. The fifty-one top vineyards – the grands crus – are planted with only the four 'noble' varieties: riesling, pinot gris, gewurztraminer and muscat."

Alfred has vines in Mandelberg and Sporen. In hot years the grapes are picked in October to make the dessert wines called 'vendanges tardives'. In years of climatic perfection, botrytis-affected grapes wither on the vine before being made into the lusciously sweet 'selection de grains nobles'.

WINES

Domaine Horcher,
Alsace Pinot Gris
Alfred's Cuvée Sélection, from old pinot gris vines, has seductive, floral and spicy aromas and an opulent texture; you can match it to the kind of savoury dishes more usually reserved for red wines. Full bodied and fresh, it goes well with Alsace specialities like 'choucroute' or 'flammeküche', the delicious Alsatian version of pizza.

Wines €4.55–€30

Irène Horcher
Domaine Horcher,
8 rue du Vignoble, 68630 Mittelwihr
- Rooms: 2 gîtes for 5,
  €415–€510 per week.
- Meals: Restaurant 5 minutes walk.
- Closed: Sunday afternoons.
- +33 (0)3 89 47 93 26
- www.vin-horcher.com

CHAMPAGNE

CHAMPAGNE

More than any other region, Champagne is identified with its greatest product. The mere suggestion of drinking it elevates any occasion into a celebration. It crosses class and cultural barriers, and shows little sign of losing its popularity in the 21st century. Its history is shrouded in folklore: the 17th-century monk Dom Perignon is wrongly credited with the invention of the drink and, sadly, never said, "Come quickly! I am tasting the stars!" A 19th-century businesswoman, the Veuve (Widow) Clicquot is, perhaps, more than anyone else, responsible for Champagne's international fame. (Veuve Clicquot is now one of the Louis Vuitton Moët Hennessy group.)

The sparkling wine has only one appellation, AOC Champagne, but Champagne is a blend of different grape varieties (chardonnay, pinot noir or pinot meunier) and it can be white or rosé, bone dry or semi-sweet. There exist grand cru and premier cru classifications, vintage and non-vintage versions, and the grower or a third party can bottle the wines. Your hosts will demystify these arcane secrets! You'll learn about champagne growing and vinification, maturing and blending.

Compared to some other wine regions the geology of Champagne is relatively simple. The underlying rock is chalk, and this soft, white stone gives the wine its character. A further advantage is that it's easily excavated, resulting in the very deep cool cellars, and these are essential for the slow second fermentation that makes Champagne what it is. Another factor that affects the wine is the climate: here in the most northerly of the French wine regions it's too cold for most wine styles but perfect for bubbly. A distilled spirit called marc de Champagne and its sweet aperitif derivative, ratafia, are well worth seeking out, as are some of the still wines produced under the Coteaux de Champagne appellation.

A glass of Champagne will complement most foods, but it goes particularly well with fish. The region's fish come from its rivers and lakes and most popular are the local brochet (pike) and sandre (pike-perch). Pork is also often on regional menus. It's the main ingredient in the traditional grape-picker's soup, 'Potée Champenoise', which can include sausages, chicken, and vegetables – more of a stew, really. You'll find delicious cow's milk cheeses like the soft, nutty Chaource, named after the town in the Aube, and the pungent, creamy Langres, which can be served aflame with burning marc de Champagne.

Our properties are found in the northern part of the Champagne region on the forested hilly outcrop called the Montagne de Reims, and on the chalk downs of the Côte des Blancs. These hills, that give interest to the plains that stretch in all directions, are home to many of the most prestigious crus of the region and footpaths criss-cross their wooded depths. In this section you will chance upon a curiosity – a whisky distillery in deepest France!

On the plains there are fascinating towns to explore: Reims with its cathedral of Notre Dame, and Epernay, the capital of Champagne. Three rivers form the region's vineyards and its countryside, the Aisne to the north, the Aube in the south and, running between them, most famous for its World War I associations, the river Marne.

Champagne Pierson Whitaker

MARNE

In the Côte des Blancs the wine route leads south from Epernay past the vineyards and through the little village of Avize. Le Vieux Cèdre is almost in the centre of the town but the steep garden with its mature trees rises behind the house to meet the vineyards that crowd in above it.

This is the family home of Didier Pierson, a fifth-generation member of a champagne winemaking family, and his English wife Imogen Whitaker. The couple first met when Imogen was working in Paris: "I came to Champagne with a group of motor cyclists on a wine trip," she recalls, "and Didier, one of the hosts, fell off and damaged his bike. I had a spare seat on my pillion, and so the introduction was made!" She will still not be separated from her beloved Ducati.

Wanting to create their own champagne marque – Pierson-Whitaker – they moved to this house twelve years ago. Now they and their two children form a truly Anglo-French family, and the children, fluent in French and English, slip easily from one language to the other.

Imogen's artistic background (she studied music at Goldsmiths College) is evident in the way the house has been restored. From the high-walled front courtyard a double-curved staircase leads to an airy, black-and-white tiled hall where books and pictures, textiles and bric-a-brac compete for attention. A 19th-century oak staircase with its elegant wrought-iron balustrade leads to a first-floor landing, from which you reach the three smart bedrooms. They are large and high ceilinged with room for two to sit and relax. Conserved and restored, the polished beech floorboards, original doors and mouldings have an elegant, timeworn feel.

Downstairs is a quiet, relaxed living room decorated with photographs and paintings by talented friends and family. The adjoining dining room, looking up to the steeply sloping garden, is where your hosts' talents are revealed at dinner. Imogen creates delicious and creative dishes to match Didier's excellent

champagnes. You can sample a different fizz with each course: a pure chardonnay blanc de blancs with the aperitif and a salad dressed with flambéed Langres cheese; an elegant assemblage to accompany the main course; and a rosé with dessert. For the cheese course, which might include the "grape pickers' cheese" Maroilles, Didier serves a sweet ratafia made from Marc de Champagne and chardonnay grape-juice.

Didier divides his time between his premier cru vineyards here and the twenty-eight acres he has recently planted in the Meon valley in Hampshire. He explains, "There's little room to plant more vines in Champagne, but the climate and geology of the South Downs are perfect." To some it came as a surprise that the first French grower to set up in England is not one of the 'grandes marques', but Didier is a true pioneer. His passion is the assemblage of the traditional pinot noir and chardonnay grapes. The French wine press has praised his champagnes; one wonders what they'll make of his English sparklers... You certainly should not leave here without a couple of bottles of Didier's excellent (and very good value) Champagne Premier Cru.

WINES

Champagne Pierson Whitaker, Grand Cru & Premier Cru
Chadonnay grapes from Didier's vineyards in the Côte des Blancs create a wine with aromas of white flowers and toasted brioche. What better way to begin a gastronomic feast than sipping a chilled glass of this while preparing oysters on the half shell with a hot Champagne and caviar sauce. Don't skimp on the Champagne in the sauce.

Wines from €15.50–€24.

Imogen Whitaker
Champagne Pierson Whitaker,
14 rue d'Oger, 51190 Avize
- Rooms: 2 doubles, 1 twin, from €65.
- Meals: Dinner occasionally. Restaurant 8km.
- Closed: 2 weeks in August. 2 weeks in September. Christmas.
- +33 (0)3 26 57 77 04

Domaine Ployez-Jacquemart
MARNE

Domaine Ployez-Jacquemart is in the centre of the quiet Champagne village of Ludes, a few kilometres south of the cathedral town of Reims. The family house is a fine three-storey 19th-century maison bourgeoise whose gardens and terraces look out over the vineyards. Beneath, dug 25 metres down into the soft chalk, are ancient cellars and there, in the constant cool, wines mature very slowly; some are stored for up to twelve years.

"Quality Champagne takes time and patience," says Laurence Ployez. Low yields, manually harvested fruit and the ancient tradition of remuage (the periodic turning or riddling of each bottle by hand) make a superlative 'slow' wine.

Laurence's grandmother, herself the daughter of a family of growers, inherited the house in 1930 and created the Ployez-Jacquemart marque. Laurence came here after living in Vancouver where she worked in gourmet restaurants before returning to continue this Champagne matriarchy. She loves to entertain and one of the many pleasures of staying here is having the chance to dine exceptionally well with your hosts. For a memorable treat book the gourmet dinner: a six-course feast of classic French dishes matched with four vintage Champagnes and a fresh, fruity rosé to accompany the dessert.

There are five stylish bedrooms, each with its own decorative theme: flamboyant or ethnic, contemporary or rustic. Baroque is a large suite with a red interior and rococo touches; Savane, a little piece of Africa in the Vesle valley. Downstairs is a comfortable living room and a quiet reading room with glazed doors that open onto the gardens where silkie hens explore the flower borders. There is a sunny terrace next to the formal box-hedged lawns for breakfast, or a stylish dining room.

Ask for a tour of the winery with its hand-carved oak foudres, and descend into the labyrinth of cellars where a river of Champagne matures in up-turned bottles; Laurence is there to explain the age-old tradition of la méthode Champenoise.

He also has just over two hectares of pinot noir and pinot meunier vines on La Montagne, the chalk scarp called between the high forest and the vale of Reims. Vine growers she has worked with for years in the Côte de Blancs grow the chardonnay grapes for the assemblage. The majority of her wines come from premier cru or grand cru vineyards, but you'll not find these mentioned on the label. "In Champagne the winery's reputation counts for much more than the its official classification," she says. Certainly her rich, fruity, harmonious wines have earned Ployez-Jacquemart international renown.

If you set off on the Champagne Route your eye will be drawn by a lighthouse that stands sentinel over the vineyards. It was built as a landmark by an eccentric Champagne négociant and now houses a remarkable ecology museum. In the woods above the vineyards you'll find wild orchids and rare, twisted beech trees; on an early morning foray you might see deer or wild boar. You'll probably be drawn to spend a day in Epernay, the capital of Champagne, where millions of bottles are kept in hundreds of kilometres of cellars.

WINES

Ployez-Jacquemart, 'Extra Brut' Champagne
Premier and grand cru vineyards provide the fruit (the proportions are 60% pinot grapes and 40% chardonnay), Madame Ployez-Jacquemart transforms the mix into this ripe, complex and balanced wine. Its elegant flavours call for a refined, yet rich, fish dish like fillet of turbot with a hot Champagne sabayon and spinach mousseline.

Wines from €21.50

CHAMPAGNE
Ployez-Jacquemart
EXTRA QUALITY
BRUT
Ludes — France

ÉLABORÉ PAR
PLOYEZ-JACQUEMART 51500 LUDES - FRANCE
NM 238.001   PRODUCE OF FRANCE

Laurence Ployez
Domaine Ployez-Jacquemart,
8 rue Astoin, 51500 Ludes
- Rooms: 5 twins/doubles, €100–€110.
- Meals: Gourmet dinner by arrangement.
- Closed: 15 December–15 January.
- +33 (0)3 26 61 11 87
- www.ployez-jacquemart.fr

BURGUNDY & BEAUJOLAIS

BURGUNDY & BEAUJOLAIS

Burgundy's fame is the result of a long association with the vine and is reflected in its architecture and landscape. The Roman conquest was secured here at the battle of Alésia and so began 2,000 years of viticulture. In the Middle Ages, the monks judged well where to plant their vines and they created the vineyards we see today. In the Yonne valley in the north and, in the south, from the Cote d'Or to the Beaujolais, the vine is king. Monastic power which created the beautiful Romanesque churches and medieval abbeys that adorn the Burgundian scenery also perfected the art of wine making. By the 15th century the Duchy of Burgundy stretched as far as the North Sea and its Flemish influence, colourfully shown in the ornate tiled roofs of Dijon and Beaune, created an international trade for Burgundy wine.

Trade, cultural exchange with other regions and a rich agricultural heritage brought gastronomy, the region's other celebrated attraction. In fine restaurants and family kitchens, French provincial cookery reaches superb heights thanks to a bounty of fresh produce: in town squares Charolais beef and blue-legged chickens from Bresse share the market stalls with Époisses cheese and wild mushrooms from the forests of the Morvan. Other ingredients, perhaps passing via Lyon in the south or the Rhinelands to the east, have made their mark on Burgundy's robust cuisine. Roman legionaries brought the vine-snail, an unprepossessing mollusc transformed with garlic, butter and parsley into escargots bourguignon. Neighbouring Switzerland gave Burgundy the fondue – a hot cauldron of red wine and herbs into which strips of beef are dipped and gently cooked. Wine's influence on the cooking style cannot be missed – you'll find coq au vin, oeufs en meurette and boeuf bourguinon, all prepared with red wine.

Starting in the north, the vineyards of the Yonne are famous for one wine: Chablis. A little red wine is made here too, in the villages near Auxerre, but this northerly outpost is best known for its flinty, flavoursome whites. Travelling south, the vineyards give way to arable fields but from Dijon almost to the gates of Lyon the vines cover a chain of hills over 100 miles long. First you enter the 'golden slopes' of the Côte d'Or, where a perfect combination of soil, climate and topography produce some of the world's finest wines. The vineyards around Nuits Saint Georges, planted mainly with pinot noir, produce most of the red grands crus; those of the Côte de Beaune to the south include world-famous whites made from the predominant white grape, chardonnay. Reds, whites and some sparkling crémant are made near Chalon-sur-Saone and in the vineyards below the limestone peaks near Macon you'll find the potently aromatic Pouilly Fuissé and some worthy reds. After Macon, the scenery becomes more spectacular as you reach the steep granite hillsides of the Beaujolais where the gamay grape makes wines of variable quality from frivolous to fabulous.

If, as many people do, you fall in love with this part of France you may want to invest in a small piece of it. Two of the wineries in the following section will rent you a row of pinot noir or chardonnay vines. But most visitors are content to come, to admire, to taste and of course to enjoy the food.

Domaine Borgnat

YONNE

There was an Iron Age settlement here. Later the Romans came, and built a temple and baths and they also planted the first vineyards. Vines still thrive on this domaine above the banks of the Yonne.

The château was built during the 15th and 17th centuries and has been in the Borgnat family for five generations. A fortified farm, the house wraps itself around a courtyard where barrels, crates and boxes of wine jostle for space with geraniums massed in pots and baskets. Queen of the castle Régine Borgnat looks after the guests. There's chambres d'hôtes in the main house; a little pigeonnier that's been turned into a gîte; and a large banqueting suite. Régine opened her doors to holidaymakers in 1990 and still loves her role as la patronne, leaving her son Benjamin and his wife Églantine to manage the vineyards and winery.

Benjamin learned his English while working in the UK. Since returning he has kept his skills honed by mingling with their English-speaking visitors and giving promotional wine tours in the States. Ask if you can visit the vaulted 16th-century cellars and sample the latest vintage maturing in oak barrels. Borgnat wines are well regarded by the experts and win prizes. "Last year we won the Tastevinage Award from the Chevaliers de Tastevin at Clos de Vougeot, and the Feminalise, a new award given by an all-female jury." Praise indeed, especially for a wine from one of Burgundy's less known (and less expensive) areas. Chardonnay vines give the fruit for the white wines, while the reds are made mainly from the Burgundy grape pinot noir, with the addition of a lesser known variety called césar or romain – names that hint at the vine's Gallo-Roman origins.

In the château you can relax in a small sitting room or just soak up the sun on the terrace as you watch the children splash in the pool. Madame is a well-travelled lady and an enthusiastic collector of bits and pieces picked up over the years. Religious, rustic, ethnic or contemporary, her objets fill

WINES

**Château d'Escolives,
Coulanges-La-Vineuse**
The Yonne valley is better known more for crisp, white wine but here is a classy red Burgundy. On the nose is a mix of concentrated cherry and prune aromas above a subtle aromatic oak. It's clean and supple on the palate with a good level of acidity and a very pleasing finish. Delicious with the russet crusted cow's milk cheese, Soumaintrain.

Wines €3.50–€9

M & Mme Borgnat
Domaine Borgnat, 1 rue de l'Eglise,
89290 Escolives Saint Camille
- Rooms: 5 twins/doubles, €60.
  2 gîtes: 1 for 2, 1 for 4,
  €240–€550 per week.
- Meals: Dinner with wine, €25.
- Closed: Rarely.
- +33 (0)3 86 53 35 28
- www.domaineborgnat.com

the house and she knows where to find the best brocante in the area. Her smallish, light-filled bedrooms lie on the first and second floors, her family suites have kitchenettes attached and the circular gîte, with its three storeys, has independent access and a small patch of garden.

After visiting the cellars and the tasting room hire a bike in the village and (without having to pedal too hard) you are rewarded with splendid views from the vineyards on the slopes of the Yonne. You could also visit the archaeological dig nearby. Lovely to look forward to a dip in the pool after a summer bike ride through cherry orchards and vineyards, and the promise of dinner at the château. Régine is particularly proud of her tasting menu, which matches a different estate wine to each course. A true polyglot, she often ends up acting as interpreter. "We usually have several different nationalities at the table and some of our specialities need explaining." Régine, forthright and charming, relishes the role. "After a couple of glasses of wine and good food the conversation – in whatever language – flows. All my guests are sympa."

La Colombière

CÔTE-D'OR

Tucked behind the town hall in the busy Burgundian village of Vosne Romanée is the maison d'hôtes of Anne Gros. Reflecting Anne's individuality, the house is far from ordinary and modern design fuses with stone, fired clay and ancient oak. Items like the state-of-the-art wood-burner and the contemporary art bring special joy in a region famous for its hide-bound traditions. This mixture of old and new is perhaps a reflection of Anne's personality: never yielding to convention, she nevertheless has a deep admiration for the winemakers who came before her. "I respect the people who created these fabulous wines," she says. "That's why I always put the name of the vineyard on the labels of my grand crus." Isn't that supposed to be interdit in conservative Côte d'Or? "Yes, but I've been getting away with it for twenty years!"

Anne abhors any snobbish associations with her beloved region so don't expect the fussy formalities of the grand château here. You enter a large, light communal kitchen where guests' names are listed on a huge blackboard. This well-equipped kitchen is a boon for those keen to be creative with local delicacies from the busy markets at Beaune or Dijon. A well-stocked fridge contains a mix of fine wines from favoured estates – a sort of grand-cru minibar. Breakfast is self-service too with baguettes, croissants and, sometimes, homemade patisseries delivered each morning.

Up a twisting modernist staircase are two large bedrooms and a family suite and, for those with reduced mobility, there's a further room downstairs, reached through the kitchen. Each room, named after one of Anne's vineyards, has its own personality: there's the muted and minimalist Les Moines for quiet contemplation and the mandarin and limestone Les Loachausse with whacky recycled sculptures. Well-planned lighting

and solid desks create a pleasant, businesslike environment in which to read or write; there's WiFi too.

It is always Anne or another family member who welcomes new arrivals and private tastings can be arranged although the list won't necessarily include the estate's own wines: demand often exceeds supply. The cellars are spectacular and well worth a visit if you get the chance. There's a small shady garden with recliners and parasols, massage and beauty treatments available. You can go truffle hunting in the forests of the Hautes Côtes or borrow bikes; Anne is a keen walker and cyclist. She suggested to a couple of guests that instead of driving to her vineyard at Clos de Vougeot they should cycle. "Before they set off they were stressed executives. When they returned they were smiling from ear to ear!"

Apart from the no-smoking and no-pets rules you'll find a list of 'reglements' on the back of the bedroom door. Translate the French and you'll realise that these are the words of the Dalai Llama. Rule number 9 could easily be Anne's credo: 'Open your arms to change but never let go of your values'.

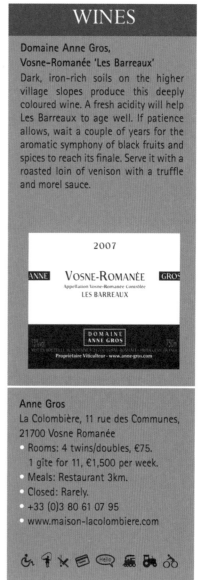

WINES

**Domaine Anne Gros,
Vosne-Romanée 'Les Barreaux'**
Dark, iron-rich soils on the higher village slopes produce this deeply coloured wine. A fresh acidity will help Les Barreaux to age well. If patience allows, wait a couple of years for the aromatic symphony of black fruits and spices to reach its finale. Serve it with a roasted loin of venison with a truffle and morel sauce.

2007

VOSNE-ROMANÉE
Appellation Vosne-Romanée Contrôlée
LES BARREAUX

DOMAINE
ANNE GROS
Propriétaire Viticulteur - www.anne-gros.com

Anne Gros
La Colombière, 11 rue des Communes, 21700 Vosne Romanée
- Rooms: 4 twins/doubles, €75.
  1 gîte for 11, €1,500 per week.
- Meals: Restaurant 3km.
- Closed: Rarely.
- +33 (0)3 80 61 07 95
- www.maison-lacolombiere.com

Domaine Lucien Jacob

CÔTE-D'OR

Is it the altitude that takes your breath away or the uninterrupted views of the vine covered hillside, the Saône valley and the Alpine peaks in the far distance? Christine Jacob intended to build a house here but practicalities got in the way and she planted vines instead. "Anyway," she says, "what better place could you imagine to plant a vineyard!"

Christine grew up in rural England and hadn't the slightest yen for viticulture. She trained as a lawyer and went to work in Hong Kong, but then she met Jean-Michel, a young French winemaker on his way home from New Zealand. They returned to Burgundy, married and raised three children. "This place has always felt like home and now I have been here over twenty years."

The vineyards share a hilly landscape of forests and meadows with Charolais cattle and working horses. "We are in the Hautes Côtes," she says gazing across the valleys below, "on the slopes high above the famous grand cru vineyards, well away from all their noise and bustle."

The winery is perched on a hillside in the pretty village of Échevronne and tucked behind the church is the Jacobs' little gîte. A perfect hideaway for two, the house is simply furnished but has all the things that count: a sunny terrace, an open fire (winter logs are free), a cosy bedroom above a rustic kitchen, and wonderful views. It's thoroughly 'old-fashioned' and all the better for it.

Visitors come throughout the year and there are wines for all seasons in the cellars. Try a delicious rosé for a summer salad or a sturdy Hautes Côtes de Beaune with boeuf Bourguignon on a clear autumn night. Proper tastings of their reds, whites and rosés, from modest Hautes Côtes or rich premier crus, take place in a cavernous tasting room cut into the rock beneath the winery. The Jacobs have 17 hectares of vines in small parcels of land here and

along the Côte d'Or. Chemical treatments have been drastically reduced and the vines are harvested by hand. Burgundy is the home of the classic aperitif, kir; four-parts of aligoté white wine with one-part crème de cassis makes the perfect drink. The Jacobs make both of these ingredients; taste their blackberry and raspberry variants, too.

Their home and export markets are thriving. "Our wines are well-known in Britain because we lease our vines to enthusiasts," Christine explains. "Guests come and stay, see their grapes ripen, learn about the winemaking process and even stick the labels on their own bottles!"

Take time to visit the medieval castles and monasteries, then picnic in the high meadows surrounded by wildflowers (try the local honey, it's exceptional) or treat yourself to a Charolais beefsteak grilled on a fire of vine roots. When the time comes to return home, buy a few bottles as a reminder of the Hautes Côtes. Better still, become one of a growing number of Brits who rent a row of vines; then you have no option but to return.

WINES

Domaine Lucien Jacob, Chambolle-Musigny

Here's the dilemma: do you wait a few years for the elegant bouquet of ripe fruit, apple, toasty oak and vanilla to develop – or enjoy the long, concentrated, juicy fruit of this Chambolle-Musigny in its youth? If you want to try it now, dish it up with a rich boeuf Bourguignon. Hide it away somewhere cool and dark and it will continue to improve.
Wines €5–€22

GRANDS VINS DE BOURGOGNE

DOMAINE LUCIEN JACOB

Christine Jacob
Domaine Lucien Jacob,
Place de l'Église, 21420 Échevronne
- Rooms: 1 gîte for 2-4,
  €300 per week.
- Meals: Restaurant 6km.
- Closed: Rarely.
- +33 (0)3 80 21 52 15

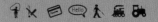

Domaine Désertaux-Ferrand
CÔTE-D'OR

Two or three vineyards away from the noise and dust of the Grands Crus wine route is the village of Corgoloin. A modest place, Corgoloin's Romanesque church and pretty vernacular buildings rarely attract the tourists who descend instead on Nuits-Saint-Georges and Beaune like an exaltation of larks. Here you miss the crowds but are in the centre of the Côte d'Or and close to the hills and forests of the Hautes Côtes. In the middle of the village is the winery of the Désertaux family who have been making fine Burgundy for over a century.

Janine Désertaux is an expert on local history and her own memories reveal much about the region's past. She recalls the armies that passed through the Côte d'Or of her childhood – first the Germans, then the Americans. She taught domestic service skills in her youth and was the president of the regional tourist accommodation committee until recently. Unsurprisingly the family's gîtes are kept in fine fettle.

Janine and her daughter-in-law Geneviève can give you a taste of the property's wines during your stay and there are always a couple of bottle for guests on arrival. The wines, delicious red and white Burgundies, win many awards.

The gîtes are named after two of the estate's vineyards. La Cabotte is a converted winery where red grapes were once macerated in bubbling vats. It shares a courtyard with Janine's daughter's house but has its own patio and a secluded garden to the side. Inside, the ancient oak beams and pale stone walls frame a sympathetic conversion.

Enclosed by a walled garden where industrious bees gather nectar from hydrangeas and lavender, Les Perrieres is reached via an arbour of vines. Escape from the summer heat within its thick walls or forget about the winter's chill and settle with a book in front of a log fire. The light bedrooms are decorated in subtle shades, floors are

clad in terracotta tiles downstairs and in shiny parquet in the bedrooms.

Modern gadgets such as electric shutters are welcome and it's a joy to find the little things that really matter at the end of a long journey: a well-equipped kitchen with basic ingredients, a decent teapot and fresh herbs growing in the garden. "We want our guests to relax when they arrive," says Geneviève. "Who wants to go shopping for coffee after a long drive?"

Many visit the Côte d'Or to sample its famous gastronomy – it's said that there is a restaurant here for every day of the year. Food apart, there's plenty more to enjoy between here and the cathedral city of Dijon, 40km away. Bicycles are provided free (a great way to discover the vineyards of the Côtes) as is all the paraphernalia for barbecues.

As a lasting memento of your stay here you can rent a row of Désertaux vines and dream of the moment when, in a couple of years, you open a case of your very own Burgundy.

WINES

Domaine Désertaux-Ferrand, Côte de Nuits-Villages
Chardonnay and pinot blanc vines produce this remarkable white Burgundy. Fruity aromatic aromas of pear, melon and banana mix with cedar, honey and vanilla. A complex and intense wine to drink with poulet de Bresse chicken cooked in white wine and with Comté cheese or with the jewel-like ham and parsley terrine, jambon persillé.

Wines €4.60–€30

Geneviève Désertaux
Domaine Désertaux-Ferrand,
135 Grande Rue, 21700 Corgoloin
- Rooms: 2 gîtes for 5-7, €450–€690 per week.
- Meals: Restaurant 3km.
- Closed: Rarely.
- +33 (0)3 80 62 98 40
- www.desertaux-ferrand.com

Les Nuits de Saint-Jean
CÔTE-D'OR

Beaune, capital of the Côte d'Or, is the epicentre of culture, commerce and wine. And it's here that France's most famous charity wine auction, Les Hospices de Beaune, takes place in November, raising funds for the ancient and venerable hospital. Hundreds of oak barrels, each containing 228 litres of wine, are sold in the market square near the harlequin-tiled roof of the town's most historic building, the Hôtel-Dieu. Quite an occasion.

In the famous wine village of Pommard, four kilometres from Beaune, lives the Violot-Guillemard family – vigneron Thierry, his wife Estelle, their teenage children and a Scottie called Tequila. Thierry was born in this small Burgundy village; today, village, house and winery have an international feel. Thierry's glorious wines are exported as far afield as New Zealand, America and Japan, while the charming chambres d'hôtes, run by Estelle, attracts an international crowd. As for Thierry, he is always on the move. Says Estelle: "one day he might be giving a presentation at an embassy dinner, and the next he's back, tending his vines. He loves to come home."

Home is this beautiful Burgundian house and its walled garden of premier cru vines. Guests stay either in the pretty ivy-covered cottage alongside the vines or in one of three large rooms in the house extension. Like most Burgundian village houses, the small street-side façade disguises a spacious interior. Plenty of floor space allows for wide beds, proper baths and big old armoires. Soft furnishings in subtle shades and limestone and colourwashed walls result in a cool, relaxed décor. There are Persian rugs on polished wooden floors and bathrooms that are tiled floor-to-ceiling.

What nicer than to take a dip in the pool by the vines as Estelle prepares an evening aperitif, perhaps a luscious Mersault. Early evening, guests meet and mingle and Estelle explains the domaine. On several scattered plots – five hectares in all – they grow both red and white varieties. "Our

WINES

Domaine Violot-Guillemard, Meursault 'Les Meix-Chavaux'
Thierry's small vineyards in Meursault have marl and chalk soil perfectly suited to the production of this superb wine. Delicate aromas of white flowers, hazelnut and vanilla prelude the creamy, buttery, palate. Try a glass of Les Meix as an aperitif, then another with tea-smoked trout fillets and a Dijon mustard, shallot and dill dressing.

Wines €6–€35

Estelle & Thierry Violot-Guillemard
Les Nuits de Saint-Jean,
7 rue Ste Marguerite, 21630 Pommard
• Rooms: 1 cottage, 3 twins/doubles, from €72.
• Meals: Restaurant 10m.
• Closed: Rarely.
• +33 (0)3 80 22 49 98
• www.violot-guillemard.fr

vines are cultivated organically and the fruit is picked by hand, so it gets rather busy in September when a dozen hungry grape-pickers gather round the dinner table."

As she chats to guests over breakfast in three languages – English, French, German – Estelle provides a spread of croissants and whole-grain breads from the village boulangerie accompanied by her own jams – try the confiture de pêche made from wild vineyard peaches. Sometimes she produces some other homemade speciality, such as a light and spongey apricot clafoutis. A big well-equipped kitchen in the cottage means you can cook your own meals if you don't fancy going out – an attractive option for a family. You can eat in the peaceful, shady courtyard with its parasols and comfy chairs, or at the long oak table – all great fun, especially if you've stocked up with fresh produce and local meats and cheeses from one of the region's markets. As for Pommard, jealously guarded by its famous vineyards, it may be small but it's bustling, charming and has a butcher's, a baker's, a small grocery and two excellent restaurants.

Château de Melin
CÔTE-D'OR

Not far from the famous Burgundy villages of Meursault and Auxey-Duresses is the little hamlet of Melin, presided over by its 16th-century château. A grand building with turrets, towers and gargoyles, its curving drive winds through wooded parkland, over a little brook (mind the ducks!) and brings visitors to a sunlit courtyard and the home and winery of the Derats family.

Hélène was born near Toulouse and after a career in technology moved to the Côte d'Or and was delighted to be accepted into village life. "Our neighbours have been very welcoming and that's the way we like to be with our guests." Her visitors come from all over the world. She finds it charming, the way her American visitors call everyone by their first name. "It's 'hey Hélène, how are you today?' – I love their informality."

After an early career in civil engineering, Arnaud Derats returned to his roots as a winemaker. "I have a collection of twenty-three hectares of vines in fifteen villages from Gevrey Chambertin at the northern end of the Côte d'Or down to Maranges in the south, where my family comes from," he says.

Arnaud is also a member of the Chevaliers du Tastevin, the berobed 'knights' of the Château de Clos de Vougeot who judge and promote the great wines of Burgundy. His wines have won many awards in France and the UK and he gives free tastings in the vaulted cellars in the ancient foundations of the house. "We rely on personal trade for a big proportion of our sales," he says. "I've never regretted broaching a bottle for a potential new customer. They always buy something!"

Hélène and Arnaud bought the property in 2000 after it had been left vacant for several years. Their structural and restoration work began immediately and balancing work on the château with running the family wine firm and raising two children was a challenge. "We worked very hard both inside the house, in the winery and in the gardens," Hélène remembers. "But somewhat against the odds we opened the first chambres d'hôtes room and received guests in September of that first year!"

The house has since been transformed and is once again a grand Burgundian chateau. It's also a genuine family home, the hub of the Derats' wine business and a successful bed & breakfast. At the courtyard level is the entrance to the underground cellars and a banqueting hall used for weddings and seminars. On the first and second floors are two large guest bedrooms and two suites, as well as the family's living quarters. Spiral stone stairways and long light corridors lead you to these very smart bedrooms. Each is elegantly furnished with well-chosen antique pieces, canopied beds, original art on the walls and Persian rugs on polished oak floors. Bathrooms are large and well built; walk-in showers and antique wash basins create a functional, characterful theme.

You breakfast at the great oval table before a magnificent fireplace where, in winter, vine roots crackle and blaze. In the middle of the Côte d'Or you're never far from a good restaurant – a mile from Melin is La Crémaillère at Auxey-Duresses and gourmets are spoiled for choice in Beaune

WINES

Château de Melin, 'Chemin de la Justice' Gevrey-Chambertin
Arnaud's Chambertin comes from a hectare of old pinot noir vines. It's matured for a year in oak barrels, a third of which are renewed each harvest. A deeply coloured, solid Burgundy bursting with blackcurrants and hint of liquorice – the classic accompaniment to the rich Burgundian coq au vin. Put one bottle in the pot and two on the table.
Wines €5–€22

GRAND VIN DE BOURGOGNE
2007
MIS EN BOUTEILLE AU CHATEAU
GEVREY-CHAMBERTIN
«CHEMIN DE LA JUSTICE»
Appellation Gevrey-Chambertin Contrôlée
DOMAINE DU CHATEAU DE MELIN
VITICULTEUR-RÉCOLTANT
13 % vol.   Paul Derats - Melin - 21190 Auxey-Duresses   750 ml

Hélène & Arnaud Derats
Château de Melin, Hameau de Melin, 21190 Auxey Duresses
- Rooms: 4: 2 twins/doubles, €95–€125, 2 family suites, €120–€150.
- Meals: Restaurant 2km.
- Closed: Rarely.
- +33 (0)3 80 21 21 19
- www.chateaudemelin.com

Domaine de l'Europe
SAÔNE-ET-LOIRE

"In the air, you're in perfect harmony with nature," says balloonist Guy Cinquin. "Every flight is an adventure and you never know where you'll end up." When keen balloonist Guy is not airborne he remains at one with nature as he expertly runs his tidy winery and two hectares of vines on the edge of the little village of Mercurey.

The Domaine de l'Europe is home to Guy and his Belgian artist wife Chantal, whose colourful murals line the walls; she also runs a gallery in the village. Upstairs, there is a small double bedroom and a compact apartment set aside for balloonists, wine buyers, grape pickers and all who wish to explore the pretty Côte Chalonaise countryside. Douglas fir from Guy's family farm in the Beaujolais furnishes the bedrooms' floors, the light from a little ivy-bordered window in the double dapples the limestone walls, and the apartment, agreeably functional, has a kitchenette and a

double bed on the mezzanine. Outside are a shady patio and a crystalline pool. Your quarters may not be sumptuous but they're comfortable, spotless and share a big white-tiled shower room between them. It's the Mercurey wines that make Domaine de l'Europe special.

Guy's two passions express his love and respect for the natural world. His homespun ecological system of viticulture minimises the use of chemicals and helps maintain healthy disease-resistant vines. He believes that "the more chemicals you use the more resistant the pests and diseases become." And, by taking the tractor into the vineyards only four or five times a year, he reduces his consumption of fuel. Guy also works at offsetting the balloon's carbon footprint (all those canisters of propane gas) by touring the vines on a bicycle.

The grapes are harvested by hand and delivered using sleds made from old barrel staves.

The fruit is macerated in enamel-lined vats for four to five days before being fermented, which adds depth of flavour and colour. A slow fermentation and a year or so in oak barrels results in a rich, well-balanced wine. Guy is dedicated to the unhurried approach. "Slow fermentation results in the kind of wine I want to make – concentrated, complex and aromatic, and not too dominated by the oak."

A full tasting of the domaine's wines has to wait until after a flight. Weekend winds and weather permitting, Guy tows his balloon, 'Le Père La Grolle', to the nearby lake, fills it with hot air, and invites passengers to clamber aboard. An hour's flight transports you over woods and vineyards in a magical silence. Your unforeseen destination could be a field of cows or a row of vines – but Guy inspires utter confidence (he's walked away with national and European ballooning prizes). After landing with a soft bump, you'll help gather acres of silk, then be treated to a glass of chilled Crémant de Bourgogne. A tasty and generous supper back at the house, accompanied by the estate's red wines, will make a soothing end to an exciting day.

WINES

Domaine de l'Europe,
Guy & Chantal Cinquin, Mercurey
Mercurey is the most important wine village in the Côte Chalonnaise. Guy's deeply coloured, structured wines are good examples of the appellation. Seventy-year-old vines on clay-limestone soil produce a rich wine with a mix of ripe fruit and aromatic oak. Try with 'queue de boeuf vigneronne', a rich oxtail stew, slow-cooked with red wine and grapes.
Wines €7.20–€12

Chantal & Guy Cinquin
Domaine de l'Europe,
7 rue du Clos Rond, 71640 Mercurey
• Rooms: 2 twins/doubles, from €60.
  1 gîte for 4, from €450 per week.
• Meals: Breakfast €7.50.
• Closed: Rarely.
• +33 (0)6 08 04 28 12

Château de Messey

SAÔNE-ET-LOIRE

White Charolais cattle slowly graze among the meadow flowers, silvery fish bask under the mirrored surface of the mill pond, the river Natouze runs gently past and time stands still in this fine old stone château and its 200 acres of woodland, pasture and vineyards. Above, a single tower stands over the home farm, the mill, millrace, pool, dovecote and pretty vine-workers' lodgings. These buildings once housed a self-sufficient community producing bread, meat, vegetables and wine. Much has changed over the centuries and now the cottages contain four delightful guest apartments.

Tiptoeing between the rare wild orchids that bless the lawns in front of the house, Vinciane Dumont relates Messey's recent history. "We moved here in the late 1980s and began by restoring the old château and its 16th-century vaulted cellars. Our priority was to modernise the winery and produce our own Mâcon wines." Success came quickly and they expanded their activities by purchasing grapes from viticulteurs in the Côte d'Or, 50km to the north. "Bringing the grape harvest back to Ozenay was tricky so we bought a second property in Meursault." Between the two venues over thirty award-winning wines are produced.

The apartments and chambres d'hôtes are managed by the Dumonts' family friends Delphine and Markus Shaefer. Charming, multi-lingual Delphine has a background in hotel and catering so the welcome is backed up by excellent cooking and a sense of professionalism. Three of the B&B rooms are in the Shaefers' cottage, in the eaves but light and spacious. The two best rooms are in the château itself, on the first floor with lovely high ceilings (one with a 'crow's nest' mezzanine) and big windows opening onto fields and vineyards. Surrounding a shady courtyard are the charmingly rustic gîtes, each named after a Burgundy wine, the largest with their own terraces.

Flagstone floors and huge stone fireplaces add gravitas, as do the heavy oak beams and pale limestone walls. Wooden beds, splashes of colour, pale walls, painted ironwork chairs, Persian rugs and gingham bedspreads bring a simple oh-so French rustic elegance.

Seventeen hectares of chardonnay and pinot noir vines are grown here within the tiny appellation of Mâcon-Cruzille. Grapes are carefully hand picked and, following a rigorous process of vinification, produce beautiful red and white burgundies. Whites are fermented in small wooden barrels and then matured in larger 400-litre foudres; reds begin life in large vats and then mature in barriques for a year or so. Such careful barrel ageing produces wines with subtle, elegant oak aromas that are easy on the palate.

Early medieval architecture and Romanesque churches, priories and castles are a reminder of the mighty monastic power that once governed these lands. If broad views and clear blue skies are more your thing, then there are some wonderful peaks to climb such as the nearby Mont Saint Romain.

WINES

Château de Messey,
'Les Avouries' Mâcon Cruzille
A green-gold robe and an intense, complex bouquet of peachy fruit and hot buttered toast come from the chardonnay vines of Les Avoueries. Ripe and fruity on the palate yet bone dry, serve it at 12°C as an aperitif, or with a fermier goat's cheese. Richness and power make it fit for the famous regional classic, escargots à la Bourguignon.

Wines €9 to €48

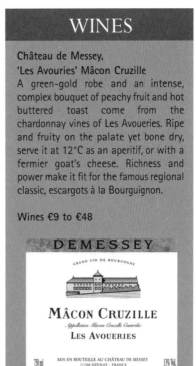

Delphine & Markus Schaefer
Château de Messey, 71700 Ozenay
- Rooms: 5 twins/doubles, €90–€120.
  4 gîtes for 2-6, €245–€740 per week.
- Meals: Dinner €30. Wine €7–€10.
  Restaurant 2km.
- Closed: Occasionally.
- +33 (0)3 85 51 16 11
- www.demessey.com

Domaine Guillot-Broux

SAÔNE-ET-LOIRE

The beauty of Cruzille is beguiling. The gentle hills covered in deciduous forests, the pale pink limestone houses capped with red pantiles, the meadows and vineyards and winding country lanes have captivated legions of visitors.

Tessara Thomson fell for its charms some ten years ago while staying at her parents' house after she finished university. She fell, too, for her future husband, Emmanuel or 'Manu'. "I was helping out with the harvest when I spotted him and I asked one of the grape-pickers where he was staying. He replied, rather gruffly, that he was staying in his room where he always did. He was the son of the winemaker, you see." A romance ensued, after which Tessara took off for a year to Tibet before they were reunited in 1999. Since then they have been developing Domaine Guillot-Broux's reputation as one of Burgundy's best-kept secrets. Their wines are truly organic: the vines have been

certified as 'agriculture biologique' since 1991 and now in the winery the addition of sulphur and sugar is restricted to an absolute minimum. Tess now finds that her palate is finely tuned to the presence of sulphur in other wines: winemakers are allowed to add up to 150mg of sulphites per litre but at this Domaine the usual amount added is only 15-20mg.

Manu asserts that the secret of the Domaine's success is the ideal geology of the higher slopes and, certainly, his white wines are impressive: every bit as rich, buttery and toasty as the classic white burgundys of Côte d'Or. The reds too are a real surprise: dark, concentrated and lightly oaked, quite different from the light, fruity wines usually associated with the gamay grape. "Wine is made from the soil," says Manu. "The grape variety is less important than the soil and," he jokes, "I'm going to produce a new wine

WINES

Domaine Guillot-Broux, 'Beaumont' Mâcon Cruzille

Manu's Beaumont vines are grown on marl-rich limestone soils on the Bathonian hills. Rigorous organic viticulture and diligent wine-making result in a remarkable red Burgundy. A rich bouquet of red fruits and violets, spicy oak and musky animal aromas will repay patient cellaring. Serve with roast pheasant and a dark red wine reduction.

Wines €8-€56

Tessara & Emmanuel Guillot
Domaine Guillot-Broux, Le Bourg, 71260 Cruzille
- Rooms: 1 gîte for 5, €340 per week; €180 weekend/mid-week.
- Meals: Restaurant 2km.
- Closed: Rarely.
- +33 (0)3 85 33 29 74
- +33 (0)3 85 33 23 87
- www.guillot-broux.com

called '100% Terroir' and see if people can guess correctly what's in it!"

Guests stay at a pretty, two-bedroom gite just over the road from the winery. There are ancient beams, limewashed walls, colourful curtains for cupboard doors, natural flooring and a wood-burner. Tess's love of the East is reflected in shyrdak fabrics from Kyrgyzstan while Manu's dedication to low-tech living is manifested in the lights made from old barrel staves. "We don't like to throw anything away," he says commendably. Outside is a small covered veranda beneath which Manu is creating a vine-hung shady patio.

The couple live a mile of so from the winery with their two sons and dogs and horses. Tess can advise on local rides and stables, and walkers and cyclists are spoiled with the range of craggy peaks and rolling limestone hills; the winery is one of the suggested stop-off points on the regional hiking route. A short distance along the broad Saône river is the medieval town of Mâcon – a lively alternative to the bucolic tranquility of Cruzille. If you can tear yourself away, that is.

La Source des Fées

BURGUNDY

A hand-painted sign on an old barn door announces that you've arrived at La Source des Fées. But instead of an air-conditioned reception area, you'll find chickens and ducks scratching in the gravel of a shady courtyard and Naya (a French bulldog of a certain age) who trots out to greet her latest friend. Close on her heels will be one of the hosts, eager to welcome a new visitor to this impressive maison d'hôtes.

Winemakers Thierry Nouvel and Philippe Greffet bought the buildings in 2002 and began a four-year restoration project. "Much of our produce is sold direct and so the chambres d'hôtes project was a natural extension of our wine business," recalls Philippe. "The work was hard, though; the earliest parts of the building are 13th century and the main batisse, built in 1656, had been empty since the mid 1970s." Batisse, in its pejorative sense, means 'old pile', but don't be fooled by this and the rustic farmyard touches: from the restored timber and stonework to the immaculate soft furnishings, antiques and collectibles, the restoration works have been carried out to a very high standard.

Upstairs, the two rooms, whose shuttered windows open to reveal views of the vineyard slopes, are larger than most Parisian apartments. Where another couple of rooms could have been squeezed into the layout, Thierry and Philippe have created a large, light salon where guests can relax on comfy sofas, read, or even play the piano (Philippe is a musician as well as a fine winemaker). Bread and croissants are brought each day from the village for breakfast and the artisan jams and apple juice are produced locally.

Sitting beside the age-old spring that gave this place its name, it's hard to believe that the busy town of Mâcon is just four kilometres away, as is the TGV railway station on the main line from Paris. Guests arriving by train can spend a couple of days here without needing a car; instead you can get around on a hired mountain bike and there's a good restaurant in the village.

Around six o'clock, the third member of the team, Gérald, invites guests to sample the excellent wines in the next-door salon de dégustation. Expect the unexpected: the Pouilly Fuissé matured in barrels is made not from oak but from acacia wood. Chardonnay and gamay grapes from ten hectares of vines harvested by hand go to make the estate's wines. "We are one of only a handful of producers here who harvest the grapes manually," Gérald says, which means they need a lot of labour at harvest time. "We announce the date of the harvest on our website; everyone's welcome to come and pick grapes with us and help to create the new wine."

After mountain biking through the steep vineyards or picking a few hundred kilos of grapes, book an ayurvedic massage, said to balance the body's energies, relieve stress and ease muscle pains.

Visit the estate's little shop where you can find interesting (and non-perishable) delicacies such as handmade chocolates flavoured with 'confit de vin' or 'peche de vigne' confiture and, of course, the estate's wines.

WINES

Domaine la Source des Fées, 'Acacia' Pouilly-Fuissé
New acacia wood barrels confer the lovely deep gold colour and a remarkable aroma to this truly modern Pouilly-Fuissé. Mineral, citrus-fresh and honeyed, the wine begs to be matched with roast duck drizzled when warm with acacia honey. Serve the duck with a mixed green leaf salad tossed in a light, honey-sweetened vinaigrette.

Wines €8-€30

LA SOURCE DES FÉES
2007
MÂCON FUISSÉ
Clos des Naïades
Appellation Mâcon Fuissé Contrôlée
Vin de Bourgogne
Produit de France

Thierry Nouvel & Philippe Greffet
La Source des Fées,
Le Bourg, Route du May, 71960 Fuissé
• Rooms: 2 twins/doubles, €115-€145.
• Meals: Restaurant 1km.
• Closed: Never.
• +33 (0)3 85 35 67 02
• www.lasourcedesfees.com

Domaine de la Chapelle de Vâtre

RHÔNE

The French verb 'dénicher' is often used when describing the discovery of a gastronomic secret. Frequently heard, not easy to translate... but for something to be worthy of the word, it should be of unique quality, not widely available and, best of all, great value. There are many French wineries that fulfil all three criteria and one such is La Chapelle de Vâtre, which crowns the top of the hill above the Beaujolais village of Jullié.

A monastic hospital was founded here in the 12th century and, later, a large farm grew from its ecclesiastical foundations. In 1996 the Caparts arrived to find the place in a sad state of abandon. After four years of restoration, the ancient farm buildings now contain the family's home and a modern winery. In two separate wings are a fabulous gîte, with panoramic views of the vineyard slopes, and three beautiful chambres d'hôtes rooms. Madame Capart, a fine-art lover, fills the rooms with abstract paintings, fun sculpture and modern collectibles. Previously a financier and industrialist, Monsieur is pouring his energy and enthusiasm into this life-changing project. In doing so, he has created a remarkable wine.

By the U-shaped courtyard you'll find the B&B rooms: Fleurie, with independent access via a huge arched doorway; and, through a shared entrance leading to a low flight of stairs, St Véran and St Amour. Linking modernism with tradition, the natural fabric of the building (exposed beams, stone walls, quarry-tiled floors) is embellished with a varied décor: bold colours here, pure whites there. Abstract paintings and pop-art prints dot the walls illuminated by halogen lights strung onto tensile steel cables. Bathrooms are thoroughly modern and delightfully spacious.

Across the courtyard, up an external spiral staircase, is the gîte. It has a huge living space, a bedroom and bathroom at either end, and a wall of glass the length of the room

guaranteeing a breathtaking panorama. From the courtyard, a sunken pathway tunnels under the house and climbs up to the little chapel at the summit of the estate – and a pool in blissful isolation. More delights? There are numerous celebrated restaurants hidden among the villages, and a network of hiking trails that pass by.

In the little winery below, or in the tasting room where breakfast is served (try the grape jams), the friendly in-house team present the estate's wines. If your experience of Beaujolais wine is of a light, fruity drink then the perfumed rosé and concentrated villages wines will surprise you; preconceptions will be cast aside when you sample these elegant oak-aged wines.

Over centuries the medieval chapel that gave this estate its name has served many purposes. Today it is a sanctuary for art exhibitions and is a sentinel whose pealing bell announces the end of the village harvest. Above all, it is a beacon to the visitors who delight in having 'déniché' this gorgeous place.

WINES

Domaine de la Chapelle de Vâtre, 'Vieilles Vignes' Beaujolais Villages
Ancient gamay vines grown on the slopes overlooked by Dominique's tasting salon produce a red wine worthy of the name Burgundy. The wine matures to produce complex aromas of ripe black fruits and spices and a smooth, balanced palate. Serve it with roasted quail and a sauce made from the juices, a handful of redcurrants, and a splash of Beaujolais.

Wines €5–€7

Dominique Capart
Domaine de la Chapelle de Vâtre,
Le Bourbon, 69840 Jullié
- Rooms: 3 twins/doubles, €70-€95.
  1 gîte for 4, €400-€580 per week.
- Meals: Restaurant 5km.
- Closed: Rarely.
- +33 (0)4 74 04 43 57
- www.vatre.com

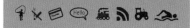

Les Hauts de Chénas

RHÔNE

Chénas, the smallest of the Beaujolais Villages crus, owes its name to the oaks ('chênes' in French) that covered these hills until the time of Charlemagne. Today, a herringbone patchwork of vines ascends from the valley floor to the highest slopes and all that remains of the once great forest is a small wooded hilltop called Les Hauts de Chénas. Nathalie's grandfather built a winery here in the 1970s and created this cosy auberge and stylish chambres d'hôtes, known as the Eagle's Nest.

A steep winding lane from the village brings you to a place where the senses are seduced, by the tinkling of goats' bells and the susurrous breeze in the pine trees. Discretely apart from the little restaurant are the guest rooms – two facing the panorama of the Saône valley and the Beaujolais hills, three at the back, with sheltered lawns. The mineral-rich soils that give Nathalie's wines their identity also identify each room. Choose between rustic, contemporary or traditional. There's Argiles in warm reds with antique oak and walnut furniture; zen-peaceful Granite in modern, muted tones; light bright Ocres with valley views. Sleek, contemporary bathrooms have big Italian showers or corner spas; Sables has a claw-foot bath.

The landscape will tempt you onto three marked footpaths that pass close to Les Hauts; they range from a three-kilometre stroll to a more sporty eighteen-kilometre hike. "We have a baggage forwarding system, too," says Nathalie. This friendly cooperation between B&B owners is much appreciated by all.

Nathalie's granddad, Emile Robin, was a noted chef. Nathalie inherited his Chénas vineyards but it was his culinary legacy that was the inspiration for opening the auberge in 2003. "Papi's passions were wine and cooking and he wanted to bring both together here. I've realised his dream and on the menus we have included some of the specialities

that won him a Michelin star in 1955." Regional dishes like 'jambon persillé' and 'andouillette à la ficelle' go well with the estate's wines. Ater all, the man who created the recipes planted the vines.

Nathalie manages five hectares of vineyards at the Domaine des Brureaux just down the hill. Chénas wines are not as celebrated as they were in the 17th century – the King of France would serve nothing else – but the appellation produces some worthy complex reds from vines up to eighty years old. Nathalie captures the personality of her vineyards in a range of wines, from light and fruity to rich and complex.

In the old vat room you get a glimpse of 19th-century winemaking. There's a huge collection of interesting artefacts but the star of them all is the storm cannon on the terrace. This device was used in the hope of dispersing hail-forming clouds whose icy precipitation could destroy the crops; when the viticulteurs realised they didn't work the cannons were discarded. Delightfully, this one survives.

WINES

Domaine des Brureaux, 'Cuvée Tradition' Chénas
A complex terroir of sandy soils above a subsoil of schist and granite allows the gamay grapes to express their full aromatic potential: the fine, clean fruit has a hint of spice and a twist of cherry tobacco on the nose. Keep it for five years or so, or drink it young with duck à l'orange. It's also delicious with desserts made from berry fruits, caramel or chocolate.
Wines €5.50–€9

DOMAINE des BRUREAUX
Chénas
Appellation Chénas Contrôlée
Cuvée Tradition 2007
Mis en Bouteille au Domaine
Nathalie FAUVIN - Viticultrice à 69840 Chénas
PRODUIT DE FRANCE

Nathalie Fauvin
Les Hauts de Chénas,
Hauts de Chénas,
Bois Retour, 69840 Chénas
- Rooms: 5 twins/doubles, €80-95.
- Meals: Dinner €17-€22.
- Closed: Mid-December to Mid-February.
- +33 (0)4 74 06 76 31
- www.levinaufeminin.fr

Domaine des Marrans

RHÔNE

South of Mâcon, leave the main road behind and wind through country lanes and delicious countryside. The route leads you on a tour of the Beaujolais villages, from Saint-Amour to Juliénas, Chénas and Moulin à Vent. After the little town of Fleurie, look out for a weather-gnarled winepress: this marks the boundary of Domaine des Marrans. The buildings may seem a tad austere but any concerns will be immediately dispelled by your hosts' welcome and the magical views – of the vine-braided hills and the misty-blue Beaujolais peaks.

Jean-Jacques inherited the house from his parents who worked the land 'en metayage': a system of sharecropping that allowed those without land to raise vines. Since taking over in 1970, and acquiring land nearby, this one-time tenant farmer now owns twenty hectares of top-quality vines. Together with Liliane and their eldest son Mathieu, he produces over 100,000 bottles of elegant

Beaujolais. Mathieu learned more about his craft in New Zealand and Australia and presents his wines with passion – the rustic Chiroubles, the floral Fleurie, the mineral Juliénas. "We cultivate the grapes naturally, using minimal treatments against disease," says Mathieu. "Rather than spray the vines indiscriminately we let nature tell us when to treat. It's a simple and cheap method that's better for the environment and the wine: a sticky pheromone-impregnated card attracts the moths whose larva damage the crop. If the moth count is below normal levels no chemicals are used."

Liliane has arranged the accommodation cleverly. You stay in one of two converted buildings flanking the main house. Facing south with views, on a clear day, to the Alps is the first-floor apartment. "We wanted to be as flexible as possible in our approach," she explains. "You can rent the whole apartment for a week or a weekend, or stay

just one night in the B&B rooms." In the larger annexe a double and a twin share the first floor above a well-equipped kitchen and dining room. Modern décor, light oak floors and (in the larger annexe) underfloor heating provide a very comfy base.

In the morning, the breakfast table is laid with local delicacies: homemade gâteaux, grape jam for hot buttered toast and (on high days and fête days) hot, sugared doughnuts called 'bugnes'. For lunch Liliane will send you off with 'le mâchon', a Mâconnais version of the ploughman's lunch consisting of charcuterie, bread and cheese (much as the silk weavers of Mâcon once ate) and a bottle of fruity Beaujolais. The silk trade is long gone but the culinary traditions continue. In the evening, head for the village and choose between the informal bistro La Bascule or the famous cuisine of the starred Le Cep, owned by the charismatic Madame Chagny.

With ski resorts to the east and Provence to the south, the Beaujolais is often overlooked by tourists but come here to discover the landscape and return home with wine knowledge that goes way beyond the frivolities of Beaujolais nouveau.

WINES

Domaine des Marrans, Fleurie
Vines of nearly 50 years of age grown on the granite soil surrounding Les Marrans give this wine its finesse and a subtle bouquet of flowers and red fruit. A clean, soft, elegant palate calls for poultry or feathered game. Try it with roast duck – the bird's dense richness is perfectly cut by the fruity acidity of the wine.

Wines €4.25–€13

Liliane & Jean-Jacques Mélinand
Domaine des Marrans,
69820 Fleurie
● Rooms: 4 twins/doubles, €55.
  Self-catering option available.
● Meals: Restaurant 1km.
● Closed: Rarely.
● +33 (0)4 74 04 13 21
● www.domainedesmarrans.com

Domaine Baron de l'Ecluse

RHÔNE

A small winery with a big reputation perches on top of the côte, surrounded by the vines and the beauty of the Sâone valley. Domaine Baron de l'Ecluse is a very special property cared for by amiable and cultured owners, Chantal and Jacques. They host concerts here in an amphitheatre and receive groups of wine tourists, cyclists and walkers; they make excellent wines, too.

The winery and its vines have passed through the female line of Chantal's family; she inherited the estate in 1994 and, with Jacques, began a long and fruitful campaign to promote the wines and the region.

"We began by putting our efforts into selling our wines direct to the customer, then concentrated on the tourism and cultural side of the domaine," says Jacques. Chantal explains how the social events have gathered their own pace. "Even in the depths of winter the mild climate

encourages outdoor gatherings. Before Christmas is the festival of lights and in summer we host jazz concerts, theatre productions, cabaret and music."

The pinnacle of the annual cycle is in November when the harvest and the year's vintage is celebrated. The feast begins with a hot meal of local saucissons cooked in the dark purple wine and continues into the starry Beaujolais night.

Groups of up to a dozen or more can stay in the stone farmhouse whose blue-shuttered façade faces a breathtaking view of the Beaujolais hills. Your hosts have created a holiday home full of colour and comfort; the mood is relaxed and perfect for a large group that wants to do its own thing. There's a large, light salon, a cosy dining room with a state-of-the-art wood burner, and an oak-beamed kitchen with all the kit needed for cooking for a crowd. Upstairs, the smart double and twin bedrooms are light and bright and there

WINES

Domaine Baron de l'Ecluse, Côte de Brouilly

Hand picked and hand sorted grapes from the high slopes of the Brouilly côte create wonderfully ripe, black fruit aromas in this sturdy Beaujolais, packed with sunshine. A mouth-filling, spicy palate with a pleasant medicinal quality call for a hearty dish. Great for a Sunday roast with crispy parsnips.

Wines from €5–€10.

Chantal & Jacques Gojowka Pégaz
Domaine Baron de l'Ecluse, Le Sigaud, 69460 Saint-Etienne-la-Varenne

- Rooms: 1 gîte for up to 15, from €750 per week;
  1 gîte for 4-6, from €650 per week, €400 per weekend.
- Meals: Restaurant 2km.
- Closed: Rarely.
- +33 (0)4 74 03 40 29

are bunk rooms for the kids. Couples and smaller groups may prefer Chantal's smart little gite in the nearby village of Odénas with its eclectic, flamboyant interiors and wonderful pool overlooking the vine covered valley.

Chantal is a member of an all-female group of winemakers who, between them, represent and promote the twelve crus of Beaujolais. "Wine is part of culture," she avers, "it is an important part of a meal shared with friends and an evening of music and dance." A lawyer specialising in wine law, she describes herself as part winemaker, part advocate – she loves the wines of Beaujolais with a passion and has even defended them in court.

Her Beaujolais wines are versatile: the frivolous Beaujolais nouveau, the crisp chardonnay, the elegant 'vins de garde' (wines for ageing) cannot fail to inspire. Jacques's reds are full of juicy ripe fruit when young, and mature well. Learn more about their making in the cool interior of the cuverie where the artistically painted vats – surely the most decorative fermenting vessels in the region – tell the domaine's fascinating story in pictures.

Domaine de la Garenne
RHÔNE

On the vine covered hillsides below Mont Brouilly is a wine estate owned by a charming and dynamic winemaker. Marc Goguet finished his army service in 1971 and returned to his roots, between the banks of the Saône and the Beaujolais hills. "I arrived with 100 francs and built La Garenne from scratch," he says with pride. In the early eighties he constructed the house and winery near the village of Charentay. Nearly thirty years later he's still building: three new gîtes have been unveiled.

Marc and his wife Christiane run the wine business, aided by their two grown-up daughters Nathalie and Isabelle. All share a fervent enthusiasm for the wines, and for Beaujolais. Well before the move into wine tourism, Marc would delight in showing his visitors round the Domaine. "Now with the gîtes we can give people more than just a sip of the latest vintage. Staying for a weekend or longer allows a real taste of the area," says Nathalie.

The three gîtes are clustered together a little way from the winery. From a south-facing courtyard the eye follows the vines over a patchwork of gentle slopes down to a wooded vale. In the distance, between the sea of green and the azure sky, rise the misty peaks of the Beaujolais hills. Back inside, these cool contemporary interiors are deceptively spacious. The well-equipped kitchens and bathrooms are decidedly high-tech while the exposed timbers and country furniture soften the new-build neatness. The smallest gîte has a large bedroom above its light living space on a curving mezzanine. For bigger parties, the two larger gîtes are ideal: La Tour with its two doubles and a children's room full of bunks, and Les Colonnes, with a huge living area and a colonnaded terrace overlooking the vines.

Thirty-five hectares of vines surround the property and everyone gets involved. Marc still

finds the time to offer a glass to his visitors and his relaxed manner is infectious. Before you know it, you'll have tasted your way through several medal-winning wines. Chardonnay fans will love the whites: a honeyed yet fresh Beaujolais Blanc, and a more serious oak-aged wine that's as good as many a white Burgundy. Expressing the true spirit of the gamay grape grown on granite soils, the red Brouilly is full of mineral and fruity flavours. "Keep it in a cool, dark place for a three or four years for the wonderful bouquet to develop," says Marc, "but of course, we always enjoy a glass at Christmas time following the harvest."

The Eurostar has opened up southern Burgundy to weekend tourism. From London to Mâcon, the train takes just under five hours and the TGV station is near: a half-hour drive from La Garenne. With weekenders in mind, the Goguets make the gîtes available for as little as one or two nights. Ancient monasteries, medieval castles and hilltop chapels are a treat to discover, as are the golden-stone villages of the Pierres Dorées en route to Lyon, the capital of French gastronomy.

WINES

**Domaine de la Garenne,
'Fût de Chêne' Brouilly**
Old vines grown on south-facing granite slopes provide the fruit for this acclaimed oak-aged Brouilly. It's rich in colour, full and firm on the palate, and Marc has captured that delicious 'plums and custard' aroma of black fruits and vanilla. Enjoy it with a saddle of rabbit or even (with the un-oaked version) a Chinese-style beef in black bean sauce.

Wines €3.50–€7.50

Marc Goguet
Domaine de la Garenne,
69220 Charentay
- Rooms: 3 gîtes for 4-12, €420–€850 per week, €250–€500 per weekend.
- Meals: Restaurant 2km.
- Closed: Rarely.
- +33 (0)4 74 03 48 32
- www.domaine-goguet.com

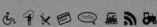

LOIRE

The Loire valley is a country of rivers and châteaux. Scores of fine country houses punctuate the watery landscape from Angers in the west to Orléans in the east. The river cuts its way through the soft pale limestone that history's château builders have quarried here since the Middle Ages. Limestone also forms the bedrock of the vineyards that give rise to the region's other famous attraction – wine.

France's longest river begins its thousand-kilometre journey in the hills of the Cévennes. The vines appear halfway along its course at Pouilly and Sancerre but here the river parts company with the vines and travels north before reuniting with the vineyards west of Orléans. From the Touraine, the Loire and its tributaries flow through a chain of wine areas: past the cave-dwelling villages between Tours and Saumur, through the misty hills and valleys near Angers and on towards the sea and the flatlands of the Nantaise.

This verdant land, influenced by the ocean's climate, benefits from warm summers and mild, if occasionally damp, winters. For centuries a region of wealth and political power, the Loire valley is famous for its wonderful examples of medieval and renaissance architecture and one or two of the places featured in the Loire section of this book are truly worthy of the title 'château'. The others, although more modest, are no less fascinating and engaging. You can spend a night in an 18th-century manor house set in hundreds of acres of parkland, or rent a cosy cottage at a winery where troglodyte caves, now used as tasting rooms, are filled with barrels, bottles and vats.

François Rablelais's 'pure Septembral juice' is a diverse family of wines. The upstream vineyards are planted with pinot noir and sauvignon blanc vines that produce light, floral reds and mineral, zesty whites. In Touraine and Anjou the chenin blanc reigns, creating sweet and dry whites (both still and sparkling) and, on the slopes above the little river Layon, a divine dessert wine. The cabernet franc grape makes the fruity, off-dry rosé Cabernet d'Anjou, and a number of aromatic, complex reds that age well. Where the river estuary meets the sea a vast area produces dry white wines and the best of them, Muscadet Sèvre et Maine, is the perfect accompaniment to a platter of Atlantic fruits de mer.

There's an abundance of fresh fish and seafood here. Fishy specialities include friture (deep-fried whitebait), pétoncles (queen scallops), brochet (pike) and matelote d'anguille (eel stewed in red wine). The Royal hunting grounds that once filled the larders of the aristocracy still produce a bounty of game; traditional peasant dishes, too, like pieds de cochon, rillettes and boudins are well worth trying. Look out for local cheese like Selles-sur-Cher and the goat's cheese crottin de Chavignol.

Our vineyard properties in the Loire are all family-owned. At each place you'll be able to taste the wines and at some you'll be invited to dine with the family. At one chambres d'hôtes the owners can take you on a tour of the region's best wineries. You'll return home with memories of fine food and wine, newly-made friends and the timeless and serene beauty of the Loire.

L'Ameline

NIÈVRE

The village of Pouilly clings to a raised côteau on the right bank of the Loire, at the midpoint of its one thousand kilometre journey to the sea. Its steep, narrow streets all seem to go riverwards. Walk down to the old quays at the water's edge and you pass the winery, cellars and maison d'hôtes of Jean-Pierre Chamoux.

Jean-Pierre and his wife Sylvie are generous, hospitable and down-to-earth. Don't expect grandeur: airs are joyfully cast aside by Jean-Pierre and conversation flows. As for the maison d'hôtes – an old lawyer's house – it stands behind the main house in a small geranium-spilled courtyard. A sympathetic eye has been used to forge three bedrooms for guests. No easy-fit skylights here, but new dormer windows to either side of the original mansard, created from local limestone. There are stone walls, oak beams, a hallway with beautiful tessellated tiles, and bedrooms that are comfortable not plush.

Do eat here: Jean-Pierre and Sylvie, keen cooks both, serve food that matches perfectly the zesty bone-dry wines. When asked what classic fish dish Jean-Pierre recommends he replies, "Oh, just some 'pétoncles' – queen scallops – marinated in orange juice with a couple of finely chopped peppers, then sautéed in a little hazelnut oil." Such understatement masks his innate understanding of the complexities of matching food with wine. The Pouilly-Fumés go equally well with freshwater fish and cheese (local, of course), but a sweet wine from further downriver is chosen to accompany the desserts. Dining with a family is the best way of finding out what the locals do with the markets' bounty.

The Chamoux's wines are fermented and matured in stainless-steel vats. They produce two wines: the flinty and aromatic Les Arables, from old vines on the higher slopes, and the fruity and fresh Chantalouettes made from younger vines. A little

WINES

Domaine Chamoux, 'Les Arables' Pouilly-Fumé
A single hectare of old sauvignon vines produce this delicate, un-oaked Pouilly. The clean, mineral and silky smooth palate follows an aromatic bouquet of pears and white flowers. Try with Jean-Pierre's suggestion of queen scallops in an ultra-light cream sauce as a delicious entrée, or with a crispy sole meunière as a main course.
Wines €8-€11

Jean-Pierre & Sylvie Chamoux
L'Ameline, 1 rue Ferdinand Gambon, 58150 Pouilly sur Loire
• Rooms: 3 twins/doubles, from €53.
• Meals: Dinner €25.
• Closed: Rarely.
• +33 (0)3 86 39 15 58
• www.ameline58.fr

vaulted cave and a few hectares of sauvignon vines are what remain of a larger wine business, some of which was recently sold in preparation for Jean-Pierre's semi-retirement. Having built a flourishing international trade, he now looks forward to running the business on a more human scale. "I now sell most of my wines directly to individual clients. I enjoy meeting old friends, and making new ones, at the many exhibitions we take part in." The region, its cuisine and its famous white wines have become Jean-Pierre's passions. He speaks French, German and English, and enjoys the social contact with guests from overseas. "Food and wine bring people from different countries and cultures together. As a meal progresses, people's experiences, ideas and dreams are shared."

Walkers can follow a number of well-marked paths along the riverside and into the wooded hills, while the regional nature reserve of the Val de Loire can be explored on foot or by kayak; get out early and you may glimpse a dam-building beaver. After a day in the hills you will return to a delicious dinner in the old lawyer's house with your appetite restored.

Domaine de l'Ermitage

CHER

Shaped by centuries of farming, the ancient province of Berry is a landscape of cow meadows and fields of barley flanked by wooded hills. Long ago the mighty city of Bourges held all regional power; its importance has waned, but Bourges has retained a gravitas with its medieval architecture, narrow cobbled streets and a fabulous gothic cathedral. Not far from the old town, on the banks of the little river Yèvre, is this 18th-century farmhouse, once a hermitage, with rich pastures where charolais cattle graze and vines thrive.

Géraud and Laurence make a dynamic couple; they are cattle breeders, vine growers, winemakers and impeccable hosts. The wisteria-covered farmhouse, set within a shady park of mature trees, lawns and colourful borders is the hub of all their activity. Far grander than a typical country farmhouse, their home is undoubtedly elegant with tall white-shuttered windows set in the creamy façade; a graceful cupola

on the steep, tiled roof; and a tall octagonal brick-and-colombage tower. Five smart chambres d'hotes rooms are split between the main house and a converted mill just across the courtyard.

From the flagstoned entrance hall of the mill, a timeworn oak staircase leads to three large bedrooms where white painted walls and pale wooden beams produce a soothing mood-lifting luminescence; country furniture and seagrass matting blend well. Breakfast (hot toast, fresh croissants and Laurence's homemade preserves) is served in a bright room in the main house, above which are two more bedrooms. All the rooms have pleasing views of the park, the lush lawns or the busy courtyard below. Daily life on the busy farm means continuous activity but, being far from the town and the main road, l'Ermitage is nonetheless a peaceful place and, apart from the odd sound of wildlife or farm, there is nothing to disturb you..

Laurence and Géraud selected nine hectares of young vines near the village of Menetou-Salon. The sauvignon and pinot noir roots delve into a seam of fossil-rich limestone called Kimmeridgian, named after the village of Kimmeridge in Dorset. "We harvested our first commercial crop in 2003 and we're still the most recent newcomers to the Menetou-Salon appellation," explains Laurence. A new wine was created in Géraud's ultra-modern winery and Domaine de l'Ermitage has since won many awards. Wines from this area are less well-known than Sancerre or Pouilly-Fumé, but are similar in style and often better value.

Bourges rewards its visitors with a millennium of history within its Gallo-Roman walls and Kafka-esque labyrinth of streets. In spring there is a festival of music and there's a summer programme of musical events.

A visit to the 12th-century cathedral followed by lunch at La Pleine Lune will nourish body and soul; students, vine workers and well-heeled locals flock to this bistro and you'll find the wines of l'Ermitage there too.

WINES

Domaine de l'Ermitage, Menetou-Salon
Géraud's Menetou wine (pronounced 'men too') is a delicious bone-dry white whose fresh peach and melon aromas complement cold starters and soft cheeses. Here in the centre of France is a wine that goes perfectly with seafood – try it with a platter of fruits de mer, plenty of garlicky mayonnaise and a crusty baguette.

Wines €5–€8

Laurence & Géraud de La Farge
Domaine de l'Ermitage,
18500 Berry Bouy
- Rooms: 5: 2 doubles, 1 twin, 1 triple, 1 quadruple, €62–€115.
- Meals: Restaurants in village or 6km.
- Closed: Rarely.
- +33 (0)2 48 26 87 46
- www.hotes-ermitage.com

Moulin de Reigny

CHER

The road from Sancerre to Reigny winds through a countryside of gentle hills where honey buzzards gyre and swoop. In the centre of the little village is the Domaine des Caves du Prieuré: a fine Sancerre winery and home to three generations of the Guillerault family. Pilgrims on their way to Santiago de Compostela once sheltered here. Les Caves du Prieuré (The Priory Cellars) are a hundred or so metres from the house. "So staying in the Priory means walking to breakfast through the village lanes," Geneviève says. What better way to begin the day?

Geneviève Guillerault and her husband Jacques have lived and worked here since 1971. Now their son and son-in-law tend the twenty hectares of vines and manage the busy wine business. Charming and courteous Geneviève looks after visitors to the winery, the bed and breakfast guests and serves delicious Sancerroise cuisine: here you eat at your hosts' table bathed in evening light from a huge arched window. The regional home cooking is a joy to share, as are the estate's citrusy whites and fruity reds. Try the Sancerre Blanc with a quiche of local crottin de Chavignol goat's cheese; the red is perfect with the classic egg dish oeufs en meurette, known here by the (perhaps less polite) regional name couilles d'âne... Madame is perfecting her English with the help of a local teacher. "I love to entertain our British and American guests," she says, "helping them make the most of their stay is perfect practice."

Across the courtyard is an ancient mill, kept as a museum, whose shadowy rooms give a glimpse of rural domestic life in the 19th century. Wine tastings and family gatherings take place here beneath the dark oak beams surrounded by mementos of the property's past. A little further, down the lane, is the Priory and its B&B rooms. A bright double in bold pink opens onto a courtyard with a spiral steel staircase leading to the first floor. Upstairs is a second

WINES

**Domaine des Caves du Prieuré,
'Les Chassenoys' Sancerre**
Grown on the clay and chalky Terres Blanches – white lands – this tiny vineyard of old vines called Les Chassenoys yields 4,000 bottles of complex aromatic Sancerre. In the intense, spicy bouquet you'll find hints of citrus and warm brioche; the palate is concentrated, buttery and long. Great with goat's cheese; fabulous with perch. Wines €8–€12

room in tranquil blue with a canopied bed; framing the room are two huge cantilevered beams whose scallop shell mouldings hark back to the Priory's connections to Saint James and the Pilgrims' Way. Back in the main house there's another double bedroom.

A tour of the Priory's cellars, deep under the winery, is concluded with a wine tasting gathered round an original oak winepress. Topped with zinc, the old press serves as a bar where Genviève fills glasses for eager buyers. After a sampling you can visit one of the many farms that produce goat's cheese. Sancerre, an historic town with Gallo-Roman origins, is a delight to explore. Its name too has Roman associations: they say there was shrine here dedicated to Julius Ceasar and that 'Saint-Ceasar' became 'Sancerre' over the centuries. In the 14th century the town was fortified and the Tour des Fiefs remains: a reminder of a once-great feudal edifice. Down narrow streets are wine boutiques and pavement cafés, and on Tuesdays and Saturdays an open-air market.

Geneviève Guillerault
Moulin de Reigny,
2 rue des Fontaines, Reigny,
18300 Crézancy en Sancerre
• Rooms: 3 twins/doubles, from €50.
• Meals: Dinner with wine, €18–€22.
• Closed: Rarely.
• +33 (0)2 48 79 01 74

Le Clos du Verêt

LOIR-ET-CHER

Bourré is a fascinating troglodyte village of vernacular stone houses built into the limestone côtes that form the Cher's northern bank. The Germain family have been making wine here for over a hundred years and now young winemaker Anne Germain is in charge of the eco-friendly winery and delightful chambres d'hôtes.

Eighteenth-century houses are full of surprises and you'll love the cellars and stairways hewn from the pale rock and the south-facing terrace overlooking the valley. Up steep steps are three rustic-smart bedrooms with high-beamed ceilings and green-shuttered windows. There's a family suite and a double whose wide balcony is warmed by the morning sun; a third double room looks out across the rooftops to the wooded hills of the Cher valley.

The house is not a château but feels like a little castle, clinging to the steep limestone cliff. On summer evenings you can dine in the cool troglodyte cave of the village restaurant – or stay here and prepare a barbecue on the terrace. There's also a shared kitchenette for guests' use. Breakfast is served at a huge solid-oak table lined with wooden benches and heaped with homemade gâteaux, preserves and fresh local produce: milk from the local co-operative, bread and pastries from the boulangerie.

The vineyards are managed using an environmentally friendly system of agriculture called 'raisonnée' (which means 'reasoned' or 'well thought-out'). Chemical fertilisers and pesticides are banned and treatments with copper sulphate are minimised thanks to a clever high-tech weather station at the heart of the vineyard. Anne explains that vines are susceptible to mildew fungus that attacks the leaves, especially in humid conditions. "With the met-station we can predict when to treat the vines and apply the optimum

WINES

Domaine des Tabourelles, 'Clos de la Salle' Touraine Malbec
You may be familiar with the dark malbec wines of Argentina or Cahors; this varietal is doing very well here in the eastern Touraine too. The deep ruby colour heralds a rich, fruity wine with black fruit aromas. A hint of liquorice and a very juicy finish call for the rich river fish stew 'matelote', cooked with a splosh of red wine.

Wines €3.50–€6.45

Anne & Aimé Josseau
Le Clos du Verêt,
9 route des Vallées, 41400 Bourré
• Rooms: 3 twins/doubles, from €58.
• Meals: Restaurant 1km.
• Closed: Rarely.
• +33 (0)2 54 32 75 51
• www.lestabourelles-leveret.com

dose." Ecological principles extend to the chambres d'hôtes: solar panels heat the water in the showers, kitchen waste is composted or recycled, goats trim the grass.

Anne believes a 'green' approach to viticulture produces a better wine. "Plants that are heavily dosed with artificial fertilisers don't need to search for the natural nutrients and minerals that give wine its flavour and aroma. You have to make the vine suffer a little to yield the best fruit." Anne's 'suffering' vines produce modern, concentrated wines from single grape varieties like malbec, gamay, sauvignon and chenin. If you like your wine based on grape variety then these will certainly appeal. Whites, both sparkling and still, are fresh and lively, and reds are supple and approachable.

Ramblers and cyclists will appreciate the numerous paths across forests and hills, while the region's medieval and Renaissance châteaux are easily reached by car. Chenonceau, the most quintessential of all, is a few minutes' drive, its fairytale turrets and graceful arches creating, in Flaubert's words, a feeling of "gentle peace, elegance and strength".

Le Clos de Fontenay

INDRE-ET-LOIRE

Near the town of Bléré by the river Cher is a little hamlet called Fontenay, a town whose history goes back two millennia. Its original château was destroyed by fire by the retreating Prussian army in 1871. Then, there was a Gallo-Roman aqueduct, a large mill and a ferry crossing over the river, which is a tributary of the mighty Loire.

The architect and painter August Bucquet built another château in the 19th century and set it in a landscape of pastures and parkland, woods and vineyards, overlooking a 'Victorian' model village of cottages and outbuildings, all in pale Touraine stone. His stonemasons engraved the words 'pax in terra hominibus' on the façade – wishes for good will and peace on earth for all who come here.

After years of neglect, the estate was bought by the Carli family in 2006. Nathalie, a sophisticated Parisienne, adores her little château and gave up a city career to oversee its restoration. "We wanted a place with vineyards that was big enough for our family and friends and not too far from Paris," she says. There are twelve hectares of vines and seventeen of gardens and woods; four chambres d'hôtes rooms and two lovely gites; and Paris is less than an hour away on the TGV from Tours. "The children love their country life and our youngest son even gives guided tours to visitors."

The restoration work was a family project and everyone rolled up their sleeves to help; one talented family member restored the stained-glass windows, some of which date back to 1532. The formal gardens are flourishing once again and, except for an area of overgrown woodland set aside for foraging deer, the grounds are beautifully manicured.

On the first floor of the château, up a grand staircase, two large double rooms have river views through large leaded windows. Antique furniture and striped or floral patterned wallpaper fit perfectly with the dark polished oak floors and the original mouldings – turn-of-the-century features that .

WINES

Château de Fontenay, Touraine Sauvignon
Didier makes two white sauvignons: an ultra-fresh wine with the sappy aroma of tomato leaves and, from grapes harvested a little later, a more ripe fruity example with notes of tropical fruits. Both are perfect partners for the Touraine's famous goat's cheese, Selles-sur-Cher – try it lightly toasted on a mixed leaf salad with a zingy vinaigrette.

Wines €4–€7

Mme Nathalie Carli
Le Clos de Fontenay,
Château de Fontenay, 5 Fontenay,
37150 Blere
- Rooms: 2 twins/doubles, €75–€125.
  2 gîtes, €500–€980 per week.
- Meals: Restaurants 2km.
- Closed: Rarely.
- +33 (0)2 47 57 12 74
- www.leclosdefontenay.com

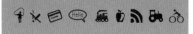

the Carlis were determined to conserve. You breakfast in the vast dining room downstairs, or on one of the terraces; fruits from the orchard and the potager go into the jams, the fresh bread and pastries come from the village.

La Closerie, originally the washhouse, is a ground-floor apartment with two double bedrooms, a smart bathroom and a light, comfortable salon with an open fireplace. There's a compact kitchen and dining area and a garden for summertime eating. In the other gîte, the handsome gatehouse at the end of the curving gravel drive, a contemporary staircase in pale beech and steel leads to two good-sized double rooms.

The winery is owned by the Carlis' friend Didier Corby who makes reds and rosés from cabernet and cot (the south's malbec), sweet white chenins, bone dry sauvignons and sparkling chardonnays. The fizzy pink Rosière, a bubbly explosion of blackberry fruit, makes a lovely aperitif.

Bléré is the home of one of France's best cheesemakers and there are many farms nearby where you can buy meat, eggs and vegetables 'at the gate'

Château de Pintray

INDRE-ET-LOIRE

At the end of a long leafy avenue of horse chestnuts is the small, intimate Château de Pintray. You will be instantly charmed by the idiosyncrasies of the place, by the curiously sail-less windmill in the courtyard and the small chapel with its twin lodge on the lawn.

The château has a documented history that goes back to the 15th century and inside you find a treasure house of curios and antique nursery pieces; in the dining room, a hobbyhorse tricycle and a Guignol puppet theatre stand alongside a billiards table. The whole place glows with personality and peculiarity yet this is no museum-piece château: Maryvonne Rault keeps five chambres d'hôtes rooms in the main house while her husband Marius has transformed the vineyards to produce some of the region's best dry and sweet white wines.

Stuffed full of character, the suites have big comfy beds on carpeted floors, family portraits and tapestries on antique papered or panelled walls, and bathrooms with huge roll top tubs and walk-in showers. There are elements that are delightfully quirky, such as sunlight shining through the cracks of a wardrobe door: peer in to find an oval window hiding behind the coat hangers. Tea and coffee are on tap downstairs but the bedrooms carry some luxurious extras like robes and lovely soaps and shampoos. For readers there are quiet corners – try the formal but comfortable drawing room, or the benches and loungers planted in shady spots in the wooded grounds.

Crossing the walled courtyard you enter Monsieur's domain: the winery and cellars. He'll give you a tour of the vines, explain the production process and talk about wine and cuisine. "They are inseparable," says Marius. "I am proud to say that my wines have been praised by some of the world's top chefs." The multi-starred Chef Patron Joël Robuchon of L'Atelier recommends a Pintray to partner his skate wing on a bed of cabbage; this accolade probably means more to Marius

WINES

**Château de Pintray,
'Cuvée des Armoiries' Montlouis**
Chenin vine roots push through metres of siliceous clay giving the nose a characteristic flinty aroma mixed with fresh citrus. Next follows an explosive mouthful of exotic fruits – lychee, mango and pineapple – balanced by a natural sweetness that doesn't cloy. Perfect with Chinese steamed sea bass covered in a hot oil of ginger and garlic.

Wines €4.50–€15

Maryvonne & Marius Rault
Château de Pintray, RD 283, 37400 Lussault sur Loire
• Rooms: 5: 4 twins/doubles, 1 family suite from €110.
• Meals: Restaurant 2km.
• Closed: Never.
• +33 (0)2 47 23 22 84
• www.chateau-de-pintray.com

than the ratings awarded by the wine press. Although vines have been cultivated here since the Middle Ages, this vineyard dates back to 1990; the château's Montlouis wines are superb. The bone-dry, medium-sweet and syrupy-sweet wines have one thing common – a juicy acidity that goes perfectly with a wide range of classic European and Far-Eastern dishes. Each year just over 40,000 bottles are produced and sold directly to private individuals and restaurants.

Business is thriving and delightful Maryvonne is constantly on the go. One moment she's serving a splendid breakfast to a dozen guests gathered round the huge dining table, the next she's off with a phone in one hand and a wad of wine receipts in the other. She speaks good English and always has time for her guests. Her knowledge of the region is invaluable if you're visiting the famous châteaux; Chenonceau, Amboise, Villandry, Cheverny, Azay-le-Rideau are all within an hour's drive.

After breakfast and a visit to Marius's cellars you'll leave with a lingering memory of a rare hospitality and some very delicious wines. Those who stay long to return.

Clos de l'Épinay

INDRE-ET-LOIRE

Half a mile from Clos de l'Epinay, the TGV from Paris hurtles through a mile-long tunnel under the limestone plateau of the Vouvray vineyards. But at the walled 18th-century manor house of winemakers Luc and Marie-Claire Dumange all is birdsong and tranquillity. The wisteria-covered house and winery wrap themselves around a courtyard behind which are tree-shady gardens and views of vines as far as you can see. Luc cultivates sixteen hectares of chenin blanc, known here as Pineau de la Loire, and his vines are tended on sustainable principles.

Hospitable Marie-Claire takes care of the marketing, speaks several languages and runs two bright, comfortable chambres d'hôtes rooms on the first floor under the eaves. Gleaming wooden floors and uncluttered furniture give the rooms a solid feel; there's an antique oak bed in one, deep blue walls in the other, and floral bedcovers and small sofas to add comfort. Bathrooms are functional, modern and spotless, with walk-in showers.

Marie-Claire nurtures her orchards with compost, and her trellised soft fruits in the walled garden produce a glut in the summer. "Visiting children love to help themselves, and everyone appreciates the homemade jams." These are served along with the usual breads and croissants in the light bright breakfast room. Luc, who took over from his father in 2000, produces a range of wine styles: dry, medium-dry, sweet, and his speciality, sparkling wine (delicious!).

Luc's fizzy wines are made by the méthode traditionnelle: the same laborious and time-consuming system that, in Champagne, turns flat white wine into an explosion of flavour. Marie-Claire is passionate about the gastronomic delights of their méthode wines. "In the Touraine, we adore these wines. And they're not just for aperitifs: you can enjoy them with savoury dishes and desserts." She pours

a foaming stream of tiny bubbles into a flute glass. "In Britain you sip sparkling wine at weddings, or smash a bottle over the prow of a ship!" Marie-Claire believes that their Vouvray complements many food styles and that Vouvray wines make a superb, often less costly, alternative to the labels of Epernay.

His combination of natural viticulture and rigorous selection are complemented by modern methods: this celebrated winery is equipped with stainless steel, thermo-regulated vats. The wines are matured in limestone 'tuffeau' cellars but Marie-Claire presents her tastings at a wooden counter held up by old oak barrels.

Vouvray is a busy little place full of wine shops and restaurants. An hour's walk through Vouvray's vineyards brings you to the majestic château of Jallanges, and the pretty village of Vernou-sur-Brenne. Further afield are the great châteaux of the Loire and the city of Tours, epicentre of the region's cultural and viticultural history. Tours has two châteaux of its own and Amboise, a short drive up river, is topped by the magnificent château of King Charles VIII.

WINES

Domaine du Clos de l'Epinay, 'Tête de Cuvée' Vouvray Brut
The Loire's most famous fizzy wine is a versatile drink from the aperitif to the dessert. Luc's Tête de Cuvée is packed with bubbles that release fresh apple and yeasty aromas. Try the bone-dry brut with a fillet of John Dory and a caviar and Vouvray sauce; the sweeter demi-sec version is a wonderful accompaniment to desserts.
Wines €6-€19

Marie-Claire Dumange
Clos de l'Épinay, 37210 Vouvray
• Rooms: 2 twins/doubles, from €65.
• Meals: Restaurant 2km.
• Closed: November-April.
• +33 (0)2 47 52 61 90
• www.vinvouvray.com

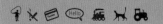

Domaine de Beauséjour

INDRE-ET-LOIRE

A fabulous property in the famous Chinon vineyards, on the limestone coteaux of the Vienne valley. Looking out onto a swathe of vines covering the whole valley, Marie-Claude Chauveau recalls there wasn't a single vine when they moved here. "Every viticulteur takes a long view, though. He plants a vineyard, he prunes, he works the soil, and all the while knows that many years will pass before it yields fruit."

Marie-Claude's husband Gérard, an architect, inherited Beauséjour from his father and planted the vines that now grace these slopes. Forty seasons have come and gone since then, the vine roots delve deep into the limestone hillside, and the fruit of the harvest makes a rich red wine. Gérard, now in his eighties, is content to see his son David continuing the tradition.

In the midst of this sea of vines lies the couple's home and their delightful bed and breakfast. The house, built in pale tuffeau stone, was completed in 1978 but its architectural style comes from the previous century. Set between the forest and the vineyards, the grand three-storey house and faux pigeon tower have an air of 19th-century elegance. Linking the two, a sunny terrace and a pool overlook the verdant valley and, behind them, a troglodyte cave makes a wonderful al fresco dining room. For guests, there are two bedrooms in the tower (one up, with views, one down, opening onto the pool), and a peaceful, very pretty two-bedroom suite on the ground floor of the main house. The interiors are bright and smart, thanks to Gérard's design flair and Marie-Claude's French good taste. You'll find mellow stone walls adorned with old prints and portraits, antique Persian rugs on black slate and, in every room, Madame's flower arrangements.

When Gérard built the house, he also built the winery – a semi-subterranean cellar in the hillside containing a huge ultra-modern vat room. Beyond the rows of shiny stainless steel vats is a gallery, 150 metres long, stocked with bottles

WINES

**Domaine de Beauséjour,
'Cuvée Tradition' Chinon**
The cabernet franc vines on the sunny,
south-facing slope yield a fruity, floral
Chinon. These wines, full of fruit in their
youth, mature well in good years to give
a rich palate of aromas. Try a young
Cuvée Tradition with the spicy French
colonial fishcake, 'accras'; the oak-aged
Cuvée Angelot is just the thing with a
roast shoulder of lamb.

Wines €5.50–€12

Marie-Claude Chauveau
Domaine de Beauséjour,
37220 Panzoult
- Rooms: 3: 2 doubles, 1 suite for 3-4.
  €70-€90; €120 for 4.
- Meals: Restaurants 5km.
- Closed: Rarely.
- +33 (0)2 47 58 64 64
- www.domainedebeausejour.com

and barrels. He restored the original 18th-century farm buildings too; here you can sample Beauséjour's award-winning Chinon wines. Marie-Claude gives an entertaining dégustation in English or French, and explains the importance of the vintage. "Our vineyard is sheltered from the north by the hilltop forest and its south-facing slope maximises the sun's warmth. But each year brings with it a unique pattern of weather that influences the wine." You'll discover, in the glass, how climate alone can create such differing characteristics.

At breakfast, plan a day's walking or cycling (a Grande Randonnée footpath passes nearby) or a tour of the local wine estates. Chinon is only ten minutes away and the 12th-century castle should not be missed; as well as the time-worn beauty of its crumbling walls, it played an important role in English, as well as French, history. For garden lovers: the Château de Villandry, whose vast potager, divided into nine equal squares, is stuffed with ornamental cabbages, radishes, peas, strawberries, sorrel, leeks, forget-me-nots and daisies, replanted twice a year. It has a dazzling beauty.

Cave du Coteau de Sonnay

INDRE-ET-LOIRE

The villages and vineyards by the banks of the river Vienne near Chinon have been home to many generations of the Baudry family. A parchment attests that the Domaine de la Perrière was entrusted to one of the Baudry ancestors six generations ago. The latest of this line, Christophe Baudry, is continuing the tradition in partnership with Jean-Martin Dutour and together they own over eighty hectares of Chinon vines. Christophe's time is divided between his commercial activities and his mayoral obligations: he was voted mayor of Cravant-les-Côteaux in 2008. His parents, Jean and Marie-Claire, manage the gîtes, and give wine tastings and tours. The excellent Chinon draws many wine enthusiasts.

One wonders if Tolkien ever travelled in the central Loire – a landscape of cave dwellings reminiscent of his hobbits' home, The Shire. Like many wineries here, the house is built from, and into, the limestone rock known as tuffeau. Beneath the house there is an original troglodyte cave where tastings take place in the warmer months. The cellars too are cut deep into the stone hillside and house many thousands of dusty bottles. Jean gives visitors a tour of the underground passages and explains how the tunnels were still being quarried well into the twentieth century.

The Baudrys' two gîtes are made from the soft, pale stone. Couples will enjoy the smaller of the two, a diminutive house perched on top of the côteau with woodland behind and a view looking down to Jean's potager and across the vineyards in the river valley below. Chinon is the birthplace of Rabelais, the monk turned writer who wrote chronicles about giants, and his books contain hundreds of local references; his character the giant Gargantua could easily have been describing Sonnay when he sang: 'On old stone, long has stood: There's the Vienne, if you look down; If you look up, there's the wood!'

Gargantuan feasts are possible in the gîtes – especially in the larger one with its immense, airy dining room; musically

gifted friends might be coerced later into entertaining the party from the minstrels' gallery. Five bedrooms have heated parquet floors and there are four bathrooms. Each gîte has its own private courtyard.

Baudry-Dutour wines are exported worldwide and win many awards so don't miss the opportunity to take some home with you. Marie-Claire begins with a rare Chinon Blanc that produces a floral bouquet reminiscent of elderflower. Next comes a Chinon Rosé which is produced 'par saignée' – by 'bleeding' the whole red grapes of their first juice leaving a juice with only the palest rose colour. The famous red wines of the property follow including the Château de Lagrille, concentrated and dark with aromas of black fruit, tobacco and a hint of liquorice.

You could launch a château-hopping tour through the Loire or choose a dedicated wine route. Chinon draws sightseers and is worth exploration before you set off. There's good fishing in rivers and lakes so bring your rods; Christophe also owns a lodge by a big fishing lake in the woods nearby.

WINES

Domaine Baudry-Dutour, 'Marie-Justine' Chinon Rosé
Vines in the Vienne valley produce the ideal fruit for this salmon pink wine. Cold fermentation produces a fresh aroma of white stone-fruit and citrus; the palate is smooth but refreshing. A delicious aperitif, a colourful alternative to white wine to go with smoked salmon, and a great match with the local goat's cheese, Pouligny-Saint-Pierre.

Wines €5–€15

Marie-Claire & Jean Baudry
Cave du Coteau de Sonnay,
11 & 12 coteaux de Sonnay,
37500 Cravant les Coteaux
• Rooms: 2 gîtes for 2-12, €380–€1,050 per week.
• Meals: Restaurant 8km.
• Closed: Rarely.
• +33 (0)2 47 93 29 68
• www.baudry-dutour.com

La Grande Maison d'Arthenay

MAINE-ET-LOIRE

Twenty kilometres south west of Saumur is a historic wine property and a delightful bed and breakfast owned by two British wine aficionados. Micaela's background is the hotel trade; Sue, a wine studies graduate, worked at the respected Sussex wine estate, Ridgeview. Their shared love of France led them to pool their skills and move to this fabulous place in the heart of the Loire.

A notary's document, written with quill and ink, tells us that the house was re-built in 1706. The cellars, hewn from the soft tuffeau rock, are earlier still and bear testament to centuries of winemaking. Surrounding the high walls of house and garden, the vast Saumur vineyards continue to thrive, but the winery was abandoned long ago. Micaela and Sue arrived in 2004, created the chambres d'hôtes, and began their wine adventure tours. "But," says Micaela, "we still make a little wine here, from hand-picked and foot-pressed grapes!"

The house is splendid: a traditional fortified farmhouse surrounded by vines, its outbuildings, bakehouse and pigeonnier forming an enclosed garden fringed with hollyhocks, irises and rambling roses. Two springer spaniels frolic; their owners, as pleased to see you, provide cups of tea and a friendly smile.

You enter a grand galleried hall where exposed stone floors and walls and great oak roof trusses create a rustic backdrop. Then it's through to the farmhouse kitchen or up to the peaceful study, via an open staircase made from an old wine press. On the ground floor are two guest bedrooms: the elegant Master with a huge stone fireplace and a garden view of the pigeon tower, and the more bucolic Mezzanine, housed in the former stables; the old hay loft creates room for an extra bed. The Bakehouse is a hideaway for two built around a bread oven, and the Vine Room has windows framed by vines.

As a teacher and qualified wine technician, Sue instinctively shares her knowledge. "We offer numerous tours,

WINES

Saumur Champigny

On a Wine Adventure tour, you will get the chance to try one of the Loire's most cherished reds. Grown on limestone hills above Saumur, it is a generous fruity wine that is served slightly chilled in almost every Parisian bistro. The wines from the best years will mature for decades – the '89s are still drinking well! Available too from their cellars.

tastings and courses. Take a one-day tour of the Saumur vineyards or set off on a lively three-day adventure. We can pick you up from the airport or train station, and you get to meet some of the region's best winemakers, many of whom have become great friends." Before the actual tour there is a wine tasting supper in the hall of La Grande Maison. The meal begins with a sweet Coteaux du Layon apéritif, then perhaps a cold entrée and a glass of sparkling Blanc Saumur. A main course, such as caramelised duck in a raspberry sauce, might be accompanied by a rich, red Saumur; and followed by a homemade dessert served with a glass of Combier, the local liqueur. "All the ingredients come from the local markets or our own organic potager."

After tasting and touring there's still much to enjoy. You can watch the sun set from the roof of the pigeonnier, settle into a good book within its tranquil interior, gaze on the vineyards or relax in the flower-scented gardens. Your hosts can even arrange a hot-air balloon flight – for a magical view of this valley of vines.

Micaela Frow & Sue Hunt
La Grande Maison d'Arthenay,
Rue de la Cerisaie, Arthenay,
49700 Les Verchers Sur Layon
- Rooms: 4 twins/doubles, €85.
- Meals: Dinner with wine, €40.
- Closed: December-February.
- +33 (0)2 41 40 35 06
- www.lagrandemaison.net

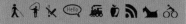

Le Manoir de la Noue

MAINE-ET-LOIRE

You wouldn't know it was there, hidden away on the edge of Dénee village, just beyond the avenues and crescents of a residential estate. Through the gates one enters another world: an old walled garden resplendent with the colours and scents of the seasons and a 16th-century manor, home of the de Cenival family. Neat paths lead to weathered statues and grottos and, at the end of a leafy lane, an unexpected moated folly introduced by a previous owner – a garden-loving academic – who restored the property with sensitivity nearly two hundred years ago.

Catherine and Olivier de Cenival discovered the world of wine after pursuing other careers; he was a software engineer, she was a restaurateur. Soon they mastered the art of wine making and in a short time have won many medals; every vintage since 2002 has earned them praise. They have also converted the former barns into a stylishly contemporary chambres d'hôtes: four bedrooms above; sitting and breakfast area below. All is comfortable and characterful: oak beams and bold colour-washed walls, big beds and generous bathrooms, with baths, showers and quarry-tiled floors. Ivy rambles across the stone façade, past pretty white shutters and up the outside stairway to the first floor.

Young vines line up in the nursery next to a newly planted mixed orchard; the older vines are to be found at the Domaine des Chesnais, Saint-Lambert-du-Lattay, a few kilometres away. The winery and cellars are also elsewhere but Olivier displays his vintages here, in the converted orangery, or even the garden. He makes several different wines: full-bodied reds; light fruity reds; dry and sweet whites; dry and moderately sweet rosés; and some 'méthode' sparkling wines. "Each wine has its character," says Olivier. "Our intervention in the vineyard and our work in the winery do not create that character, but they do enhance it." Grapes from small parcels of land are vinified in separate vats to preserve the identity of

the various 'terroirs' and confer upon each wine a sense of place. "This is why you see the name of the specific vineyard on my labels." This emphasis on 'terroir' does not mean that the vines are given over entirely to Mother Nature's care: from springtime to the harvest Olivier is focused on selecting and nourishing the best quality fruit.

Catherine prepares a breakfast of warm breads and croissants in the open-plan kitchen and dining room. The orchard gives the fruit for her jams and 'gelées' while the vineyard provides a delicious unsweetened grape juice made from Olivier's grolleau grapes. She is a great source of knowledge on this rivery region and full of ideas for places to visit. "This landscape is centred on the Loire. You can kayak and fish in summer, while in springtime the river in flood is an amazing sight." She particularly recommends the village-island of Béhuard, whose 15th-century church was once a place of pilgrimage, and then a drive up to La Corniche Angevine, a rocky promontory from which unfolds a wondrous panorama of France's longest river.

WINES

Domaine des Chesnais, 'Les Bonnes Blanches' Coteaux-du-Layon
Les Bonnes Blanches comes from a small parcel of two and a half hectares of chenin vines at Saint-Lambert. Late harvested grapes create a nectar-sweet white wine with aromas of honey, raisins and spicy oak. Creamy desserts or soft cheeses go well with the wine's sweetness; it's also good with grilled figs stuffed with goat's cheese and wrapped in Vendée ham.
Wines €3–€12

Catherine & Olivier de Cenival
Le Manoir de la Noue,
49190 Denée
- Rooms: 4 twins/doubles, from €75.
- Meals: Restaurant 5km.
- Closed: Rarely.
- +33 (0)2 41 78 79 80
- www.domainedeschesnaies.com

Vignoble Gelineau

MAINE-ET-LOIRE

In the ancient province of Anjou two tributaries, the Layon and the Aubance, join the great river Loire. Between these meandering streams is an area of vine cultivation ideally suited to making sweet wine. The pretty, hilly countryside and luscious dessert wines draw nature lovers and connoisseurs like bees to a honey-pot. Many people still harvest by hand; wineries are small, family concerns and production is low. The Gelineaus have been making wine here for generations and son-in-law Pierre-Antoine welcomes visitors to the cellars throughout the year. He's keen to promote local wine tourism and during the summer he organises vineyard walks, gastronomic events and art exhibitions.

For a week's tour of the Loire valley vineyards, or for a family get-together, Château Viaudière is the perfect base. The gîte next to the château is large, well-equipped and decorated in a simple, rustic style with some antique country furniture. In the large dining room armchairs are gathered round an open fireplace and a glazed door opens onto a sunny, sheltered patio; in the functional kitchen there are table and benches for breakfasts or informal meals. From here you go out into a sunny walled garden with views across the vines. On the ground floor is a double bedroom with its own bathroom; three more doubles are upstairs, with polished pine floors and great views, and sharing two shower rooms.

Don't miss out on a tour of the tasting salon and cellars. As your eyes adjust to the dim light, you perceive the pale ghostly figure of a knight in armour; the poor fellow has lost his sword and, holding aloft its hilt, seems to raise a toast to your arrival. Here at the tasting bar you can enjoy the honeyed, syrupy Coteaux du Layon wines and reds, rosés, dry whites and fizzy crémant too. Pierre-Antoine

Vignoble Gelineau Château la Viaudière, Coteaux de Layon
Pierre-Antoine's late harvest moelleux is sweet and fruity with aromas of quince, honey and lychee. Loire sweet wines like this all share a mouthwatering acidity that calls for rich savouries like foie gras, blue cheese or saucy fish dishes, or desserts like pear tart or apple charlotte. It might last decades – if you can wait that long!

Wines €3.40–€6.80

Pierre-Antoine Giovannoni
Vignoble Gelineau,
Château de la Viaudière,
49380 Champ-sur-Layon
● Rooms: 1 gîte for 11,
  €450–€550 per week.
● Meals: Restaurant 2km.
● Closed: Rarely.
● +33 (0)2 41 78 86 27
● www.vignoble-gelineau.com

explains, in very good English, the magical natural processes that create his sweet Coteaux wines. "On cool autumn mornings, the river mists rise into the vineyards, bringing with them the spores of a very useful fungus called botrytis. As the chenin grapes begin to wither, their sugar levels rise. The grape-pickers make several passes through the vines to harvest only the most sweetly concentrated – et, voilà: our sweet wine." The wine made by these grapes is both unctuously sweet and juicily acidic and keeps for years.

For hikers and cyclists, a number of trails criss-cross the vineyards connecting the sleepy villages. At Whitsun there's a festival of art, music and dance at nearby Rablay. Angers, the capital of Anjou, is just across the river Loire; its metropolitan centre is chock-a-block with restaurants, galleries and museums. Its castle contains the world's largest tapestry – a 14th-century depiction of the biblical Apocalypse. Another château, France's tallest, is at Brissac, only a short drive away. The 17th-century castle's seven stories, flanked by two towers, are open to all; they too have a vineyard.

BORDEAUX & SOUTH WEST

BORDEAUX & SOUTH WEST

The southwest of France, ancient Aquitaine, is a region of diverse landscapes. Its cultures and even its languages are diverse too. However, from the Basque country in the foothills of the Pyrenees to the Gironde estuary on the Atlantic coast, one custom is shared by all – winemaking.

Two mighty rivers, the Garonne and the Dordogne, have shaped the region's wine lands. Rising near the Spanish border, the Garonne and its tributaries form the vineyards of Gaillac, Fronton, Cahors and Buzet. The vine is also found further south in the Armagnac country of the Gers, the vineyards of Jurançon and Madiran, and the mountain slopes near Irouléguy. In the east, the Dordogne begins its journey in the Auvergne and follows a twisting westerly route through Bergerac and past the hills of the Duras. Where the two rivers meet are Bordeaux's famous appellations: the Médoc and Graves on the low, gravelly lands to the west and the vineyards of Saint Emilion and Pomerol on the right bank of the Dordogne. All wine styles are made here and some of the world's finest and most expensive red, white and sweet wines come from these hallowed fields.

The Atlantic climate brings warm summers (very hot inland, but cooler in the mountains and by the sea) and mild, sometimes damp, winters. Hard frosts, bringing potentially disastrous consequences for the vines, are not uncommon, but for most of the year you can eat al fresco and enjoy a taste of sunlight trapped in a bottle. Enjoy, too, the rich Gascon cuisine: foie gras, magret of duck, and prunes d'Agen are staples on many menus and these watery lands produce a wonderful range of seafood and river fish. Try a Bordelaise lamprey cooked in red wine or a platter of Arcachon oysters. Autumn chestnuts and wild mushrooms fill the market squares of the Dordogne. Bayonne ham and Cantal cheese make the simplest, most delicious of picnics.

The wine areas of the southwest have been cultivated since Roman times and Ausonius, the 4th-century Latin poet, praised the vineyards that were already well established in his day. In the 12th century, the marriage between Eleanor of Aquitaine and Henry II brought these lands under the control of the English crown, and for three centuries a flourishing wine trade developed. The Battle of Castillon, in 1453, put an end to English rule; Aquitaine was surrendered to France, but the trade continued. In the Middle Ages a lighter style of red wine was favoured and so the Gascon merchants, using the word 'clairet' to describe their clearest wines, gave rise to an English word: claret. Bordeaux's golden age began in the mid-18th century and resulted in today's beautiful architecture and the rise of its aristocratic wine châteaux. Three UNESCO world heritage sites are within easy reach of the Bordeaux vineyards: the riverside Port de la Lune, the medieval village of Saint-Emilion and Vauban's fortifications at Blaye. The Atlantic coast, the delectable Dordogne and, in the south, Gascony and the towering Pyrenees are equally memorable.

In Bordeaux, any wine property can be called a château whether it's an historic castle, a stately home or merely a residence. The winemakers here are an interesting bunch; among them are artists, chefs, musicians and the only Englishman in France distilling Armagnac brandy, proving that the historic links with Aquitaine still hold strong in the 21st century.

Château Le Bourdieu

GIRONDE

Arrive by car ferry and avoid the suburbs of Bordeaux: the Médoc peninsular is an island in all but name. Bounded by the ocean to the west and north and the Gironde to the east, the Medoc's remoteness from the city that lies forty miles south is part of its charm. The vineyards share the landscape with forests of poplar and rich pasture lands, fishing villages and ports; at Valeyrac, near the tip of this land between the estuary and the sea, Château le Bourdieu surveys its vines.

A son and grandson of vine growers, Guy Bailly acquired the property in 1978. He and his family live in Bordeaux but continue to make the very same 'cru' that was noted in the 1878 edition of the wine bible, Féret. The fabulous château that adorns the labels was built in 1830, but a map from the 1700s shows the property much as it is today, surrounded by woods and vineyards.

You can rent one of two small gîtes. One is an old vine workers' cottage facing the château courtyard and winery, with its own small lawn at the back shaded by cherry trees, bounded by a sea of vines. A recent refit has transformed the old stone building into a simple but smart one-bedroom gîte with a well-equipped kitchen, a bathroom with an Italian shower and a cosy sitting room. It's good value, too. The larger gîte is an apartment on the first floor of the main house, reached via an outside stair. An unpretentious flat for four with a 'below stairs' décor and a brightly tiled kitchen, its large windows look onto the vineyards and down to the courtyard – a sheltered spot for al fresco suppers and barbecues.

Le Bourdieu is an excellent address from which to discover this surprising region. As Guy says: "people like the diveristy. Within an hour's drive you can reach the Atlantic beaches, the great

WINES

Château le Bourdieu, Médoc

An equal mix of cabernet sauvignon and merlot grapes creates a generous wine with a ripe fruit, an attractive oak and a hint of vanilla. Smoothing out nicely from their fourth year, Guy's wines can be consumed without having to wait too long. He suggests a glass of Le Bourdieu with a rich and creamy Poularde à la Crème with morels.

Wines €8.50–€10.50

Guy Bailly
Château Le Bourdieu,
1 route de Troussas, 33340 Valeyrac
- Rooms: 2 gîtes for 4,
  €350–€450 per week.
- Meals: Restaurants 3km.
- Closed: Rarely.
- +33 (0)5 56 41 58 52
- www.lebourdieu.fr

city of Bordeaux, the famous first-growth châteaux... while here, on our doorstep, is the tranquil Médoc and nature all around." Cycling in the Médoc is a joy – no hills! A morning's ride will ferry you along country lanes, past the little seaside resort of Soulac to the port of Verdon. From here you can catch the ferry across the mouth of the estuary, or return via the coast road and watch the surfers catch the waves.

Guy's cabernet and merlot vines are a stone's throw from the Gironde. "The river and the sea have a strong influence on our climate," he explains, "and balance the temperature and humidity of the vineyard." This natural climate control has obvious benefits for the health of the vines and the ripeness of the grapes. Guy's award-winning wines are generous and complex, a year's ageing in barriques resulting in a fine balance of ripe fruit and integrated oak. Taste some at the winery, or head off to the restaurants of the city of Bordeaux; good claret it is best served with food. You can buy all you need at the huge open-air market at Montalivet, open every day during the summer.

Château Le Grand Moulin
GIRONDE

From the north, the flat arable lands of the Poitou-Charentes give way to braided hillsides as you cross the boundary into Aquitaine. The Roman province that became an English principality is now the world's most famous 'région viticole'. Better known by the name of its top city, Bordeaux, it's a vast region whose vines cover an area larger than England's Yorkshire. The first vineyards you meet are on the slopes of the Côtes de Blaye on the Gironde estuary, and if you leave the autoroute behind you're at Château Le Grand Moulin within minutes: a typical Blayais winery and a lovely, homely B&B.

Yolande Réaud welcomes you to her turn-of-the-century manor house with a cup of tea and a smile. In winter, you're ushered into the salon to sit by a fearsome stove; in summer, you can relax on the terrace in front of the charming neo-classical façade. Yolande relates the family history. "My grandfather and his father built the house in 1904.

They were industrious farmers who became wine traders and vine growers." They needed a grand house and so Le Grand Moulin was constructed: an elegant gentilhomerie with thirty hectares of vines.

Gilles and Yolande handed over the enterprise to their son Jean-François; he presides over a business that produces 150,000 bottles a year. Yolande remains in charge of the chambres d'hôtes – four double rooms and a couple of large suites on the first floor. These old-fashioned rooms, stuffed with character, continue to resist the makeover that will one day come. Beds wrapped in immaculate sheets and blankets, topped with pretty spreads and lacy pillows, are matched by muslin curtains and some of the original wallpapers. Bathrooms are large, several with antique fittings and capacious baignoires; it's truly authentic.

Breakfast is served in a small formal dining room surrounded by period furniture. Yolande makes

WINES

Château Le Grand Moulin, Premières Côtes de Blaye

The result of carefully selected sauvignon blanc grapes, macerated on the skins and fermented in oak barrels, is an aromatic, citrusy white wine with a buttery-smooth and lingering finish. An obvious choice to serve with a platter of the freshest Arcachon oysters or a roast chicken marinated in honey, lemon and rosemary.

Wines €4–€15

Gilles & Yolande Réaud
Château Le Grand Moulin,
La Champagne,
33820 Saint-Aubin-de-Blaye
• Rooms: 6 twins/doubles, from €55.
• Meals: Restaurant 1km.
• Closed: Rarely.
• +33 (0)5 57 32 62 06
• www.grandmoulin.com

her own 'pain perdu' – a hot, buttery bread sweetened with sugar, spiced with cinnamon. There are her jams, too – fig, quince, wild plum and vine peach – and no shortage of warm bread and croissants to spread them on.

The dining room doubles as a small sitting room for guests but on warm evenings you may relax outside at a table among the trees as the children play on the swings. Across the courtyard is Jean-François's ultra-modern winery; visit and taste. They produce a range of wines here, from full-bodied, oak-aged reds grown on gravelly soils to lighter reds, rosés and whites from vineyards of sandy clay. Jean-François explains the labour that his top vintages demand. "For good wine you need good fruit – simple but true! We harvest on different days to catch the fruit at its peak, then at the winery we eliminate all but those grapes at the peak of perfection." The entire family joins in and the wines win new awards with each vintage.

Come for a fascinating slice of authentic French life, staying with a family whose work expresses the passion that drove their forefathers three generations ago.

Château Bellevue-Gazin

GIRONDE

The Romans planted vines here, on the ridge of low hills above the Gironde. Several centuries later this hilltop was occupied during the Arab incursions and the vineyards still bear the name Gazin, a corruption of the word Saracen.

The Lancereaus' winery is a place of peace today and the conservatory windows take in a breathtaking panorama of the valley. In the evening the shimmering estuary reflects the vermilion sunsets that momentarily set the vines aglow. The Bellevue part of the name needs no explanation.

Anne-Sophie recalls cheerfully their search for a wine property. They wanted a hillside vineyard, not too big, with the potential produce a high-quality wine. "It also had to be a convivial place," she explains, "somewhere to host gastronomic soirées and tastings and a forum for artists and sculptors." Their search ended when they discovered this turn-of-the-century house and,

although it needed a huge amount of attention, it suited them perfectly. The vineyards and winery were put in order first, in 2007, and then attention was turned to the house.

After restoration they opened their doors to the first B&B guests in 2008. Anne-Sophie loves English antiques and in the three bedrooms, up a broad twisting oak staircase, you find pieces of restored furniture and ornate old mirrors. The walls are hung with watercolours, lithographs by artistic friends, and a series of family caricatures sketched by Anne-Sophie's movie-making grandfather. Bathrooms are large and functional and weary travellers will love the corner spa baths.

Breakfast is a generous buffet of organic cereals, fresh local bread and pastries and homemade jams. The setting is grand whatever the weather – in the grand salon in winter or out on the terrace among the hortensia in summer. The

WINES

Château Bellevue-Gazin, 'Premières' Côtes de Blaye
Perfumed and concentrated, black-fruity and subtly spiced, Bellevue-Gazin makes a wonderful food wine, but also drinks well on its own, thanks to silky tannins. A delicious accompaniment to red or white meat dishes, so be adventurous and try it with Riz de Veau à l'Ancienne (calves sweetbreads in a rich whole grain mustard sauce).
Wines €5–€13

Alain & Sophie Lancereau
Château Bellevue-Gazin,
Montuzet, 33390 Plassac
- Rooms: 5 twins/doubles, from €70.
- Meals: Restaurant 3km.
- Closed: Rarely.
- +33 (0)5 57 42 02 00
- www.chateau-bellevue-gazin.fr

rich limestone soil that nourishes the vines, by the way, also gives those hortensia flowers their distinctive pink hue.

Fifteen hectares of Premières Côtes de Blaye vineyards cover the west-facing côte that slopes towards the village of Plassac. Alain explains the mix of grape varieties that thrive here: "We grow merlot grapes for their softness and rich fruit, malbec for its wild aromas of spice and flowers, cabernet to give structure and the fragrance of crushed blackcurrants, and a less well-known varietal called 'petit verdot' to give backbone." Chemical treatments are kept to an absolute minimum and yields of wine are relatively low. "We put nothing into our wine apart from passion and hard work," says Anne-Sophie.

If the endless serried ranks of vines begin to lose their charm, there's plenty more to see and do. The Romans built impressive villas and there is one that you can cycle to. A short ride away are Bourg and Blaye; each is a fortified seaport; the latter's 17th-century citadel is a world heritage site. Also at Blaye is the ferry, le bac, which takes you across the broad Gironde to the Médoc and the high-duned beaches of the Atlantic coast.

Château de la Grave

GIRONDE

Spire-topped towers amid a sea of vines pull you towards this enchanting 18th-century château. Northwards, the limestone côtes continue to Blaye and the broad Gironde estuary; to the south, the gently undulating hills drop down to Bourg where Bordeaux's great wine rivers, the Dordogne and the Garonne, meet. A castle has stood on this lofty site for five centuries, patiently guarding a patchwork landscape of fields, woods and vineyards. The turreted façade was constructed before the Revolution, but the years since have not diminished the Château's romantic, aristocratic beauty.

Constant Bassereau bought the château in 1904 and moved here from the flat lands of the Vendée. Today, great-grandson Philippe and his wife Valérie continue the family tradition of viticulture and winemaking. Philippe manages the vineyards and the winery; Valérie takes care of the marketing, gives tours and tastings, and runs a stylish chambres

d'hotes. She recalls their entrée into wine tourism, in 1994. "We were among the first B&Bs in this region. We had no idea whether anyone would even want to stay at a winery, but as this house is so special, so unlike a classic girondine, that we thought we'd give it a try." Fifteen years on, the visitors' book continues to grow. And, in 2008, La Grave was awarded an international Best of Wine Tourism award.

Three baronial bedrooms on the first floor are packed with character; neither minimalist nor fussy, they have a mix of Louis XIII furniture and contemporary pieces. Two have balconies with vineyard views, while La Tour – the room in the tower – is a show-stopper, with its circular bathroom and canopied four-poster.

Downstairs, a flagstoned entrance sprinkled with antiques and collectibles leads you into a lordly dining room where breakfast is served under the glassy gaze of Philippe's hunting trophies; in summer

you eat on a terrace overlooking the vines. Wine tasting takes place in the magnificent 'salle de dégustation' and the small pool is ideal for an evening dip.

Above all it is a family home. "When we started, the children were small," says Valérie, "and our guests were charmed by the family atmosphere." Harvests come and go, the children have grown, but La Grave is as delightful as ever. A mock-heraldic motto in the cellars says it all: 'Ni grand château... ni petit... Château de la Grave je suis!' ('Neither grand nor small, Château de la Grave I am!'). The cellars are interesting in themselves, their oak-beamed vaults lodging shiny state-of-the-art vats and dusty old vintages going back to the 1950s.

La Grave is just over a mile from the river port of Bourg-sur-Gironde, a fortified promontory that has been home to kings and bellicose invaders for centuries. On Sunday mornings the market square bustles with shoppers in search of oysters, fish, charcuterie and cheeses. Others wander down to the much-loved brasserie, Le Café Plaisance, for hearty food accompanied by a front row view of Bordeaux's mighty river of wine.

WINES

Château de la Grave, 'Grains Fins' Côtes de Bourg

A rare assemblage of semillon and colombard grapes makes this rare white Côtes de Bourg. Citrus and peach aromas with a deep and complex palate make this an unusual and delicious white Bordeaux. Good for all stages of a meal, especially with fish, white meat and cheeses, it's a delight with a salad of seared scallops.

Wines €11–€15

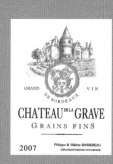

Philippe & Valérie Bassereau
Château de la Grave,
33710 Bourg sur Gironde
- Rooms: 3: 1 double, 1 triple, €75-€90. 1 family room for 4, €120.
- Meals: Restaurants in Bourg, 2km.
- Closed: February & 2 weeks in August.
- +33 (0)5 57 68 41 49
- www.chateaudelagrave.com

Château Mayne Lalande

GIRONDE

Château Mayne Lalande, a Listrac winery in the Haut Médoc, sits between the classed growth vineyards of Saint Julien and Margaux. Bernard Lartigue's family have farmed here for 150 years and he has been head of the château since 1975, when he restructured the farm to concentrate on wine production. Reminders of the mixed farm's past remain. Sheep graze the lush pasture, horses doze head-to-tail in the paddock, and coppiced woodland forms the boundaries between the vineyards.

The house is an 18th-century Girondine in golden stone and the maison d'hôtes, Les Cinq Sens, is just across the lane. Mayne Lalande is a tranquil place that indulges the senses: birdsong and rural vistas; forest scents and the touch of ancient oak and stone; and Bernard's excellent Listrac wines.

On the ground floor of Les Cinq Sens sit three large suites with contemporary bathrooms or wet rooms and direct access to the terrace behind. The vines are close by but from your windows the views are of lawns and tree-fringed paddock. In one room the vast bed is the centrepiece; in another, an original fireplace and stone sink hint at the building's age; terracotta tiles and exposed beams form a rustic backdrop to contemporary furniture. Upstairs are two more suites, each with elegant windows. All is fresh, uncluttered and super-smart.

Breakfast is laid out in the dining room downstairs, or on the lawn. For groups of eight or more Véronique, who cares for guests, can organise a déjeuner champêtre amongst the vines, cooked and served in a little cabin a short walk from the château: a memorable way to discover the domaine's wines.

The wine tour begins in the garden where Bernard has planted over fifty varieties of vines. Next, the modern stainless steel vat room and the wonderful chai. "Not the biggest cellar room in Bordeaux," he admits, "but surely the most beautiful."

Few would argue with that. The barrels, full of maturing wine, occupy a spectacular vaulted space built in oak and stone: a cathedral dedicated to Bacchus!

Mayne Lalande wines are rated as cru bourgeois supérieur – the highest rank for non-classed Médoc. Soil types suited to the two main varietals (gravel for the cabernet vines, clay-limestone for the merlots) combined with a ban on chemical fertilisers produce healthy plants. Bernard tastes the grapes each day leading up to the harvest and when the fruit reaches perfection the crop is picked by hand. The wine is ripe and wild-fruity – British Master of Wine Jancis Robinson has described it as "the ripest Listrac... all charm and pleasure".

The premier cru châteaux of Pauillac, Saint Julien and Margaux are nearby. A little further are fashionable Arcachon by the sea and Europe's highest sand dune, at Pyla. And then there's Bordeaux, forty minutes by car, notable not only for world heritage status but also for the longest shopping street in Europe, the pedestrianised Rue Sainte-Catherine.

WINES

Château Mayne Lalande, Listrac Cru Bourgeois
Wild ripe black fruits mix with toasty oak and floral notes to make a wonderful bouquet. In the mouth it's fine but structured, with a touch of spice and a good finish. Bernard makes complex wines but prefers to match them to the simplicity of honest country cooking and suggests roast pigeon to go with this worthy wine.

Wines €8–€16.50

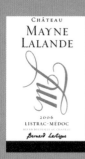

Bernard Lartigue
Château Mayne Lalande,
33480 Listrac-Medoc
- Rooms: 5 suites, €80–€180.
- Meals: Dinner only for large groups. Restaurant 2km.
- Closed: January-February.
- +33 (0)5 56 58 27 63
- chateau-mayne-lalande.com

Château Meyre

GIRONDE

Château Meyre is home to a luxurious nine-bedroom hotel, Le Clos de Meyre, set in the middle of a magnificent park and fifteen hectares of Haut Médoc vines. The château's long history is intertwined with the vigorous vine: the first castle was built in 1652 and grapevines have been cultivated here for over 300 years. When the present house was built in the late-1800s, its wines were ranked among the best in the area.

Typically French, the classical façade is delicately detailed in warm-toned ashlar. Mansard windows and strikingly slender chimneys look down to a walled garden of lawns, shingle pathways and a central pond. Beyond the arbour of roses and the cypress trees are the vineyards and a small paddock.

A charming, knowledgeable host, Isabelle Poco, director of the Clos de Meyre, has previously worked in the grand hotels of Paris and Le Touquet.

A native of Bordeaux, she is proud of its history. "There are three UNESCO world heritage sites an hour away," she tells us, "but closer still are the châteaux and their world-famous wines."

Château Meyre's owners and the friendly, professional team have embraced wine tourism. Everyone is invited to visit the state-of-the-art winery and cellars, and tastings are arranged for guests. Isabelle can also organise cookery classes and tours of the 'classed growth' properties nearby. There are bikes for hire (ride to Margaux and the Gironde estuary), a pool, sauna and tennis courts.

Named after ancient world deities, the bedrooms too are confidentially characterful. Ceridwen, named after the Celtic goddess of nature, is the largest suite and is decorated in a rich Louis XIV style, with an original marble fireplace and satin covered walls. You have a dressing room, solarium and a broad, private

terrace. There are two smaller doubles on the first floor of the main house, Floriala and Vinalia. where the opulence continues with bold fabric wall coverings.

The reception rooms are joyously flamboyant. In the entrance hall, a huge vase of flowers adorns an inlaid table, there are comfy sofas and quiet reading corners in the baroque drawing room, and a long table of polished walnut is laid for breakfast in the dining room beneath crystal chandeliers. It is a rare pleasure to find so much personality in a hotel.

In a modern wing to the side of the house are six more double and twin rooms: Maia has direct access to the gardens; the others, on the first floor, have views of the park and the pool.

In a high-ceilinged hall is the impressive tasting room and an exhibition of fairground artefacts and wine bric-a-brac. Here you can taste a ripe, powerful Haut Médoc and a rich, spicy 'micro-cuvée' Margaux. The vines are cultivated organically and in the eco-friendly winery a water recycling system and heat exchanger add to Meyre's green credentials

WINES

**Château Meyre,
Haut-Médoc**
Partially hand-picked grapes from 25-year-old vines are fermented in stainless steel and matured for six months in French oak barrels. The result is a rich aromatic claret, dominated by a ripe fruit and supported by a good balance of tannin and acidity. A good food wine, serve a bottle with slow-baked, meltingly tender confit of goose.

Wines €9–€25

Isabelle Poco
Château Meyre,
16 route de Castelnau, 33480
• Rooms: 9 twins/doubles, €90–€230.
• Meals: Restaurant 7km.
• Closed: Rarely.
• +33 (0)5 56 58 22 84
• www.chateaumeyre.com

Château du Tertre

GIRONDE

The château surveys fifty-two hectares of cru classé vines on the low hill – the 'tertre' that gives the house its name. Much has changed since its 12th-century beginnings, when it formed part of the estates of the Lords of Arsac: during the 1700s, ownership passed to Pierre Mitchell, a wealthy Irish industrialist; then to Etienne Buissière who built the Regency manor house. Inclusion in the famous classification of 1855 established Tertre's reputation and once again they make great wines. The present owners have also transformed the first floor of the winery into a fabulous collection of suites.

Since 1997, the château's destiny has been in the hands of Dutchman Eric Albada Jelgersma. A businessman, francophile and art lover, he is a passionate devotee of the region and the wines of Margaux (he's also responsible for the 3rd growth Château Giscours in nearby Labarde). His professional team, led by fellow countryman Marc Verpaalen, will put you at your ease and the welcome is as memorable and as splendid as the house.

From a tree-lined courtyard you enter the ground floor reception rooms of the winery. Honey-coloured stone walls and venerable oak ceilings evoke a timeless sense of permanence and the recent reconstruction work has not diminished the building's charm. A grand dining room leads through to the drawing room and a broad staircase to the upper floor. Here are the bright and lofty suites, furnished with unostentatious good taste. Huge roof timbers, exposed and white-painted, support high ceilings; tall windows cast a soft luminescence on embroidered bedspreads, polished antiques and magnificent paintings of the Flemish school. Joyful surprises are revealed in secret chambers: a daybed in one; in another, a huge baignoire overlooking the vines.

WINES

**Château du Tertre,
Margaux Grand Cru Classé**
Deep colour, richness and complexity, elegance and finesse – this is a classic Margaux. Aromas of ripe fruit with hints of leather, sweet tobacco and spice precede silky-smooth tannins and a satisfyingly long finish. It calls for a hedonistic dish like Tournedos Rossini – a symphony of beef fillet, foie gras and black truffle.
Wines from €18 (2nd label) & €32 (Grand Cru)

Marc Verpaalen
Château du Tertre,
Avenue de Ligondras, 33460 Arsac
• Rooms: 5 twins/doubles, from €260.
• Meals: Restaurants 6km.
• Closed: August & Christmas holidays.
• +33 (0)5 57 88 52 52
• www.chateaudutertre.fr

In the corridor that links the bedrooms there's a superb drinks cabinet for guests (a sort of cru classé minibar) but for an introduction to the wines you must take a tasting tour. Three separate halls house the different types of vat – oak, steel and new concrete – and, on two subterranean storeys below, is the vast barrel cellar where the wines rest in oak barriques. From the cellars you re-emerge into a smart tasting salon.

At the tasting table, Marc's easy-going yet impeccable style cannot conceal his passion for these deeply coloured, complex wines. Made from a blend of cabernet, merlot and a touch of petit verdot, the estate's second wine, Les Hauts du Tertre, is fresh and spicy. "The spice comes from the petit verdot. Like a single clove in a dessert, you only need a hint to make all the difference." The top wine, Du Tertre, is ripe and rich with a firm structure and an aromatic complexity that makes each mouthful a moment of discovery.

Afterwards, head for the peaceful Côte d'Argent with its high sand dunes, lonely forests and the Lac d'Hourtin, the largest lake in France.

Domaine de Valmengaux

GIRONDE

"The previous owner kept chickens in the wine vats," says Vincent, as he recalls the state of the cellars in 2000. "But the vines were healthy and we released our first vintage in the millennium year." Vincent Rapin chose the name Valmengaux for his new wine, a contraction of his children's names: Valentin, Clementine and Margaux. And to complete the family venture, Vincent's wife Béatrice, an architect and interior designer, restored the 18th-century winemaker's cottage that flanks the vineyard. Domaine de Valmengaux was born, a noteworthy micro-winery, an ecological vineyard and a delightful gîte.

Béatrice is the daughter of a Saint-Emilion wine family but Vincent left a musical career (as a jazz bassist) to work with the vines. He loves these tranquil vineyards, which he describes, entertainingly, as "right in the heart of things but miles from anywhere." Galgon is far from the posh appellations of the Médoc and Saint-Emilion but right in the middle of Bordeaux's Right Bank. Béatrice adds, "guests who stay tell us they really appreciate the peace and quiet."

The honey-coloured stone cottage has been thoughtfully renovated and, with three double rooms and a children's room with four bunks, it is perfect for two families. Floors are of stripped pine or brick, the stone fireplace has been revived and the oak beams painted in pale colours. Outside is a small pool with a changing hut and a kiwi-covered pergola which in January hangs with ripe fruit. In spring and summer there are peonies and roses and, in the orchard, plums, figs, pears and walnuts.

You're welcome to visit the winery and taste the excellent red Bordeaux, but the winemaking process does not encroach; both vat house and cellars are discretely separate from the gîte. Vincent's ecological principles led him to install natural light wells in the cellars and a heat exchange system to maintain temperature and humidity

WINES

Domaine de Valmengaux, 'Bordeaux'
Classified simply 'Bordeaux' the wine is far from ordinary. Hand-picked fruit from old vines on limestone-clay slopes create a ripe plummy wine with bags of aromatic oak. Drink Vincent's wines young or keep them in the cellar; broach a case at Christmas – the spicy, oaky bouquet and sturdy body are fit for roast goose or turkey.

Wines €25–€30

Béatrice & Vincent Rapin
Domaine de Valmengaux,
8 Petit Gontey, 33330 Saint-Emilion
- Rooms: 1 gîte for 10,
  €500–€1,400 per week.
- Meals: Restaurant 10km.
- Closed: Never.
- +33 (0)5 57 74 47 17
- www.valmengaux.com

levels. His vines may not be classified as organic but he produces a thoroughly natural wine. "What we search for, above all, is balance," explains Vincent. "Artificial fertilisers destroy the balance of the soil so that the vine can no longer find the nutrients and the minerals it needs." He reintroduces microbial life to the soil by ploughing between the vines, and plants new hedgerows to encourage flora and fauna. "In this way we create a healthier and more natural life cycle – and, hopefully, a tastier wine." These are modern, silky wines and they're enjoyed young. Valmengaux wines are seldom found in the UK so make sure you take a few bottles home.

From the hills above the Dordogne you can follow the valley road to the Périgord-Limousin Park, where natural beauty and 'a thousand and one castles' await. Then return to Valmengaux as the sun sinks below the vine-braided hills, for a barbecue and a bottle of Vincent's wine. "Don't serve it too warm," says the ex-bassist, "nor too chilled – just... cool."

Château Richelieu

GIRONDE

Cardinal Richelieu, in a quest to acquire the best Bordeaux vineyards, purchased lands here on the hill of Fronsac. France's most powerful man was a devotee of the grape and is famously quoted as saying, 'If God forbade drinking, would He have made this wine so good?' His grandnephew inherited the château and introduced Fronsac wine to the royal court at Versailles. It's said that Marshall Richelieu's favourite mistress lived here and the estate's finest wine, La Favourite, is named in her honour.

There has been a château on this land since 769 and today's classical petit château is in the care of Arjen Pen, a Dutchman who left the airline industry to pursue his winemaking dream. The oldest part of the house, the 17th-century chartreuse, has a dining room and a smart, formal drawing room; tall, elegant doors open onto lawns. The guest rooms are in an 18th-century wing and are named after characters from Dumas' 'The Three

Musketeers'. Athos, Porthos, Aramis and D'Artagnon are up twisting stairs; on the ground floor is Richelieu, named after the Cardinal, the Musketeers' wicked archenemy. Large, elegant and unfussy, the rooms are furnished with fabrics that complement the colourful walls and the shiny dark floorboards. Huge bathrooms are spoiling, with modern basins, marble tops and gleaming chrome.

In the gardens you'll find quiet leafy glades, clipped lawns and a part-walled swimming pool surrounded by evergreen shrubs. You can breakfast here when the sun shines or, during the winter months, within the thick stone walls of the chartreuse. At the far end of the building are the cellars and a little boutique where Arjen gives tastings to overnight guests and visitors.

Beyond the château's grounds, covering the southern slope of the estate, are Richelieu's vineyards. "From Roman times these vineyards

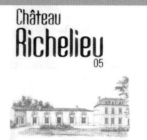

WINES

Château Richelieu, 'Grand Vin' Fronsac

Clay and limestone soils on south-facing slopes produce a classic claret with concentration and freshness. Richelieu is rich and dark with a superb balance of fruit and oak. Make a bottle the main event during a meal starting with goose rillettes followed by roast guinea fowl 'vigneron style' (with a grapey sauce). To finish, a mature Cantal cheese.

Wines €10–€20

Arjen Pen
Château Richelieu,
1 chemin du Tertre, 33126 Fronsac
- Rooms: 5 twins/doubles, €80–€100.
- Meals: Dinner €42, by arrangement.
- Closed: 24 December–2 January.
- +33 (0)5 57 51 13 94
- www.chateau-richelieu.com

were reputed to be among the best in the region," says Arjen, "but during the last century Fronsac's popularity declined. The terroir retained all its special properties and from the 1980s people rediscovered the qualities appreciated by the ancient winemakers. The subsoil, the south-facing slopes and the estuary's microclimate make this exceptional land."

Many have praised Arjen's wines and his talented team. Rich and concentrated, the wines are aged in small barrels for a year after which the tannins and oak are silky-smooth. Multi-starred chef Alain Ducasse selected Château Richelieu for his restaurant in Tokyo, and Robert Parker, the American wine guru, awarded 93 points out of 100 to La Favourite. Quite something.

Learn more about Fronsac wines at the Maison du Vin; after, drink a glass with the locals at a riverside restaurant. Walking in the hills you'll discover Romanesque churches and glimpse fine views across the river Garonne. Or take a tour of the Fronsac wineries. "You are given a 'passport' that is stamped at each address," says Arjen. "Get enough stamps and you could win a magnum of wine. Could there be a better souvenir?"

Château Pierre de Lune
GIRONDE

Saved by a couple of kilometres from the tourist crowds and the traffic of Saint-Emilion, is a small winery with a big wine. Château Pierre de Lune, deep among the vast, manicured vineyards of its classed growth neighbours, seems proudly isolated. The château, once just an old stone farmhouse but now grander, and embraced by tree-shaded lawns and vines, is the winery and chambres d'hôtes of Véronique and Tony Ballu.

By Bordeaux standards the property is tiny, but each year a single hectare of organically cultivated vines produces 3,000 bottles of Saint-Emilion wine. This small-scale production means you can experience viticultural life at close quarters and sleep, literally and happily, above the vats.

The couple live in Saint-Emilion but Véronique, a cultured, genial Parisienne, is always there for her guests. "People love the tranquillity here," she says. "The town is so busy in summer but here you're surrounded by nature."

From the gardens a large arched doorway opens to a handsome reception room. Dinner is served in this high-ceilinged space that once housed a sleeping army of barrels. Véronique cooks delicious evening meals with wines to match each course. A salad of Aveyron sheep's cheese might be followed by magret de canard, grilled over a fire of vine cuttings – a fitting match for Tony's grand cru reds. You can have breakfast here too, or take it on the south-facing lawn in the dappled shade of the hackberry trees. On the ground floor is the largest of the bedrooms, furnished in a simple country style with a canopied bed, antique oak furniture and a checkerboard, terracotta-tiled floor. There's a large, contemporary shower room and upstairs are two double bedrooms with polished pine floors. Windows onto the garden let in the sunlight and the evening chorus of nightingales.

Born in the Champagne region, Tony feels that winemaking is in his blood; he also works as technical director at the 'classé' winery, Château Clos Fourtet. "The land we found here in 1999 has the potential to produce a very fine wine. Even our first harvest was a great success."

The couple both studied viticulture and oenology and the result of their expertise has brought praise from the world's wine commentators. With only a small parcel of vines to cultivate, Tony's hands-on approach can afford to be painstaking. "We prune the vines using the 'guyot simple' method leaving only six or seven buds on each stem. In July we 'green' harvest quite rigorously – during ripening we prune the foliage to reveal the grapes to the sun." Pierre de Lune has been described as a 'vin de garage' and it's easy to see why. A single stainless-steel vat is housed in the winery next door to the tiny cellar, just big enough for twenty barriques.

It's a five-minute drive to Saint-Emilion or Libourne where you can cross the Dordogne and venture to the grand old city of Bordeaux and its magical quayside, the Port de la Lune.

WINES

Château Pierre de Lune, Saint-Emilion Grand Cru
The wine has a beautiful carmine robe and unveils aromas of ripe blackcurrants and spicy oak in perfect harmony. It's concentrated and structured, but with an elegance and subtlety that call for a refined dish. Try Pierre de Lune with medallions of beef in a wild mushroom, truffle and red wine sauce, or osso bucco with a black truffle risotto.

Wines €5–€41

Veronique & Tony Ballu
Château Pierre de Lune,
3 Magnan, 33330 Saint-Emilion
- Rooms: 4 twins/doubles, €50–€100.
- Meals: Dinner with wine, €40.
- Closed: Rarely.
- +33 (0)5 57 24 68 12
  +33 (0)6 70 80 24 27
- www.chateau-pierredelune.com

Château Franc Pourret

GIRONDE

Close to Saint-Emilion, encircled by five hectares of organic vines, is the home of the Ouzoulias family. Limestone gravel crunches underfoot as you draw up to the main house – a classical pale-stone petit château complete with pediment and portico.

The house, vineyards and winery are fastidiously well-kept. Catherine's son François, now in charge of winemaking, has a passion for organic production that has earned Franc-Pourret organic status as well as grand cru classification. When asked about his approach to winemaking François is emphatic that organic husbandry is the best option. "Five generations of the family have been here making and selling wine since 1889 and we feel we are part of the land. That is why we choose not to use harmful chemical treatments." Does la viticulture biologique require more effort? It does, but François believes it is worth it.

"We plough and harrow between the vines instead of using herbicides, and encourage the grass to grow, to retain moisture and nutrients," explains François. "We use natural manure and organic compost when the soil needs feeding and, to deter parasites, use remedies made from nettle and seaweed." As if to demonstrate just how excellent the soil is, François points at the lamb's lettuce growing between the immaculate pruned rows of cabernet and merlot vines. "Voilà! My mother can grow salad leaves in this soil even in winter." The carefully-nurtured grape crop is harvested and sorted by hand and the whole family joins in. If you fancy picking a few hundredweight of grapes, then time your visit for September.

To stay is a treat. Catherine has created two lovely large bedrooms on the first floor at the top of a swirling banistered stair, and furnished them in formal Borderlaise style. There are gleaming antique armoires, upholstered chaises longues and big comfy beds on new wooden floors. The rooms are well thought-out so there's heaps of space and good lighting; warm red walls in one, mellow yellow in the other, and

WINES

Château Franc Pourret,
Saint-Emilion Grand Cru
The vineyard is planted with an equal
mix of old merlot and cabernet franc
vines on limestone slopes west of Saint-
Emilion. Expect heady aromas of
blackcurrant and apple, vanilla and
liquorice. The palate is ripe and soft but
with a structure and acidity balanced by
the fruit that will allow this wine to age.
Try with entrecôte Bordelaise.
Wines €13.50–€16.80

Catherine Ouzoulias
Château Franc Pourret,
33330 Saint-Emilion
• Rooms: 2 twins/doubles, from €79.
• Meals: Restaurant 1km.
• Closed: Rarely.
• +33 (0)5 57 24 72 29
• www.ouzoulias-vins.com

shutters to protect you from the quiet-at-night road.
Bathrooms too are roomy and well-equipped. This is a
breakfast-only chateau but a twenty-minute walk through
the vines brings you to smart restaurants and lively
subterranean bistros in Saint-Emilion: there's heaps of choice.

You can visit the cellars and winery and, just above, a little
museum of viticulture; artefacts have been collected by the
family over the years. Afterwards indulge in a private tasting of
François's wines – the atmosphere is relaxed and friendly. The
property's top wine, Château Franc-Pourret, best demonstrates
the efforts put in in the vineyard and the cellars. The wine is left
to mature for a good twelve months in small French-oak barrels.

The next day, stroll down to breakfast at little round tables
prettily laid by the fire or, in summer, on the terrace with
vineyard views. Catherine serves her special 'winemaker's
breakfast' on request – a feast of locally cured charcuterie,
fresh eggs, homemade jams and, every day, some extra
homemade delight. There's an unusual addition to the spread:
a glass of Franc-Pourret wine.

Château Monlot

GIRONDE

Between Saint-Emilion's limestone côte and the Dordogne river sits this beautiful 18th-century winery in seven hectares of grand cru vines. Its little courtyard is a peaceful place, and its tranquil, leafy gardens are a delight to return to.

Bernard and Béatrice Rivals, the amiable owners, succumbed to Monlot's charms in 1990. Beatrice was born into a family of winemakers but Bernard, an industrialist, was new to this world. He swapped manufacturing for wine-making and became a successful vigneron – none of which had occured to him before he met Béatrice. "If I'd fallen for a butcher's daughter, I'd be making sausages today!" he jests.

Château Monlot is a fine example of a typical 'maison girondine'. The living areas, barrel cellar and vat house are all contained within its pale limestone walls and, although the family no longer lives here, the house has a welcoming feel. Photographs from travels – mostly Bernard's in the Far East – share the walls with family portraits and memorabilia. Exposed stone, ancient armoires and original fireplaces add an authentic feel and the French-traditional theme stops just short of being flamboyant.

The Aliénor suite is decidedly opulent with its canopied four-poster and deep sofas. There are four further double rooms on the first floor, all large, all with garden or vineyard views. The largest, with lovely tall windows, is Semillon, and all bathrooms come with bath and shower. Downstairs you'll be drawn to a hearthside sitting area on cosy winter evenings and a courtyard in summer, part-shaded by a hundred-year-old magnolia. The striking dining room is a perfect example of the Girondine style: high oak-beamed ceilings, honey-stone walls, terracotta floor tiles.

A winery tour with Bernard begins in the semi-subterranean cellar where the wine is matured in a mix of

WINES

Château Monlot,
Saint-Emilion Grand Cru
A rich, black fruit is complemented by a toasty oak – the result of a careful maturation in new French barriques. The palate is both fresh and firm but this merlot dominant Saint-Emilion can be enjoyed in its youth with a côte de boeuf. Keep it in the cellar for a few years before trying it and the complex bouquet will astound.

Wines from €18

GRAND VIN DE BORDEAUX

Château Monlot

SAINT ÉMILION GRAND CRU
APPELLATION SAINT-ÉMILION GRAND CRU CONTROLÉE

S.C.E.A VIGNOBLES RIVALS

MIS EN BOUTEILLE AU CHATEAU

Bernard & Béatrice Rivals
Château Monlot,
St Hippolyte, 33330 Saint-Emilion
• Rooms: 5: 4 doubles, 1 twin,
  €85–€130.
• Meals: Restaurants 2km.
  Guest kitchen.
• Closed: Rarely.
• +33 (0)5 57 74 49 47
• www.chateaumonlot.com

old and new barriques. After a visit to the vat rooms and a stroll among the vines you return to the house for a taste of grand cru reds. There are two cuvées – a vat-aged Tradition and a barrel-aged Prestige – and Bernard may treat you to a comparative tasting of two or more years. As in every French region, each year's weather conditions creates the vintage's character.

Much of the estate's wine is sold direct and Bernard travels to exhibitions all over France. "The chambres d'hôtes business is a natural extension of the wine business," he says. "We like people to stay a while, enjoy being with us, discover more about our wines and experience the true nature of Saint-Emilion." Monlot's wines receive many medals and the visitors' book is full of praise.

Pretty hilltop Saint-Emilion is only three kilometres away – visit its ninth-century monolithic church, miraculously carved from within the limestone cliff. Then pass by the bell tower for a guided tour: starting in a hermit's cave, it ends with a glorious panorama of grand cru vines.

Château de Pitray

GIRONDE

On 17 July 1453 the French army defeated the English at Castillon and put an end to the Hundred Years' War. On the eve of battle the English troops had plundered the cellars of a local priory and helped themselves munificently to the barrels they found there – so much, it would seem, that we can presume the French victory was secured with a little help from the wines of the Côtes-de-Castillon. A few kilometres north of the battlefield at Pitray stood a feudal castle whose name has survived six centuries of history. They make wine here, too.

You travel down a shady avenue of trees until, suddenly, a fine vista of house and parkland comes into view. Follow the curving drive and you arrive at the neo-gothic château, resplendent in its coat of Virginia creeper, surrounded by acres of woodland and vast sweeping lawns. Château de Pitray is the family home of the Count and Countess de Boigne, whose forebears came here 600 years ago. Pierre-Edouard and Alix look after the guests during their stay and their son Jean now manages the vineyard.

As she leads you to your quarters, through gothic arch doorways and up spiral stairways, the Countess points out the many old maps and family portraits that illustrate the history of her ancestral home. The first house on this site was built by the Ségur family in the 17th century; the current one was built in 1868. On the second and third floors, reachable by lift if you don't fancy the stairs, are four suites, each with a big bathroom attached, and a side room with extra beds. They're attractive rooms, generously proportioned and comfortably traditional, some with dressing areas, others with writing desks, all with polished floorboards and elegantly upholstered furniture. Light pours in through stone mullioned windows, and uninterrupted views, of parkland, woods and fields, stretch for miles.

Dress up for dinner! It's served in a grand dining room lined with 18th-century oils and sprinkled with oriental mementos from an adventuring ancestor. Benoit de Boigne was favoured by princes and emperors during the wars in India

WINES

**Château de Pitray,
'Madame' Côtes-de-Castillon**
Rigorously selected fruit, fermented and
matured in oak barriques, gives a Côtes
wine of concentration, elegance and
complexity. Fruit and spice on a long
finish call for rich red meat and game
dishes. Roast saddle of venison with a
wild mushroom forestière sauce would
make a suitably lordly dish to serve with
this grand estate's wine.

Wines €6–€15

Pierre-Edouard & Alix de Boigne
Château de Pitray,
33350 Gardegan
- Rooms: 4: 1 double, 3 suites,
  €150–€200.
- Meals: Dinner by arrangement.
- Closed: November–March.
- +33 (0)5 57 40 63 81
- +33 (0)5 57 40 63 35
- www.chateaupitray.com

and Jean tells us how another of his forebears was presented
with the Admiral de Suffren's coat-of-arms from the stern-
castle of his flagship. "Fortunately, we have the room to
display it!" Looming over the long dining table, the carved
motto proclaims: 'The Lord will provide.' Breakfast is served
more intimately in the Belle Epoque morning room next door;
below are the château's vaulted cellars, reputedly haunted.

Outside is a terrace overlooking a large pool – irresistible
in summer – and you have the estate's 100 hectares to roam.
You can go cycling nearby or canoe on the Dordogne. Jean
also gives tours of the winery and a tasting of the wines. "The
Côtes-de-Castillon is in fact an extension of Saint-Emilion's
limestone plateau," he explains. "Our established merlot and
cabernet franc vines grow in much the same excellent clay-
limestone soils." These conditions, and the rigorous work in
the vineyard and winery, result in a wine of elegance, finesse
and complexity. If the Pitray vineyards stretched just five
kilometres to the west in Saint-Emilion, the wines could sell
for double the price. Be sure to go home with at least a case.

Domaine de Naujan

GIRONDE

On a rocky promontory overlooking the Dordogne valley is a castle set in seventy hectares of vines and forest. The Lords of Naujan built this fortified manor house at the beginning of the 14th century at a time when Aquitaine was under English rule. The château outlived the Naujan dynasty, surviving wars and revolution, and remains today a beautiful reminder of 700 years of history. Not only do you get bags of historic charm, but the panoramic views across the vineyards to the distant hills are wondrous.

Frédéric Batisse, whose father acquired the château in the 1960s, is Naujan's present guardian. He is a master stonemason and built the modern winery within the old walls, revitalised the vineyards, and restored the ancient buildings to create a superb hotel and restaurant.

The hotel's name honours Lady Isabeau, a 17th-century countess who, having no heir, was destined to be the last of the Naujans. Isabeau de

Naujan is a small, elegant, family-run hotel with twelve smart rooms and a restaurant.

The large, walled courtyard is presided over by the grand three-storey house. Mullioned windows look out from a pale, unadorned façade crowned with a roof of red pantiles. On the left are the winery buildings; on the right, the restaurant and terrace. Behind the house is the pool and a splendid view of the valley. The double or twin rooms are in traditional style and decorative features add a personal touch, like the grape motifs and the vine leaf finials. Polished wooden floors, oak beamed ceilings and antique armoires give a glimpse of Naujan's past.

Play French billiards or simply relax in the baronial lounge, a sociable room with rich red sofas gathered round an impressive stone fireplace. Meals are served on the terrace or in the restaurant across the courtyard. Naujan's creative chef always

WINES

Château Lafleur Naujan, Bordeaux Supérieur

Beautiful dark colour with a purple rim. A delicate nose of crushed strawberry and cherry mingling with withered flowers (roses and lilac) and spices (coriander, pepper), the well-structured palate combines harmoniously with the fruit and the spice. A good finish ends on the floral notes. Lovely wine, delightful with a leg of lamb or jugged hare.

Wines €3.80–€12

cooks with local ingredients; Madame Batisse, a devotee of fine dining and fine wines, loves to see her guests enjoying both. "Eating at a winery is the best way to discover its wines," she says. "Here, the estate's produce is in the kitchen, as well as on the wine list!" Try the pavé of beef with new season beetroot cooked in red Bordeaux.

Prior to 1998 when the winery and cellars were modernised, the grape harvest was sold each year to a cooperative; now Frédéric makes, bottles and sells his own wine and Naujan's reputation is building. The chateau's thirty-eight hectares, planted with the five classic Bordeaux varietals, produce bone-dry whites, sweet dessert wines, fruity rosés and supple reds, and you can take part in a tutored wine/food matching course.

You can pedal off into the gently rolling hills in search of limestone caves and ruined castles. The historic hilltop town of Saint-Emilion is just over the river, as is the site of the battle of Castillon where, in 1453, the French army finally defeated the English after 300 years of occupation.

Mme Batisse
Domaine de Naujan,
33420 Saint-Vincent-de-Pertignas
- Rooms: 12 twins/doubles, €80–€150.
- Meals: Dinner €16–€35.
- Closed: 15 December–February.
- +33 (0)5 57 55 02 86
- www.domaine-de-naujan.com

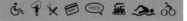

Château de Claribès
GIRONDE

In rolling hills a few kilometres from Sainte-Foy-la-Grande is Claribès, an enchanting place, not isolated but away from the summer crowds. Hoopoes call from the tops of the trees, the river Soulège babbles through the valley; and Stone Age artefacts from limestone tunnels beneath the pigeon tower suggest that people lived here well before the Romans first planted the vines.

"It's a far cry from Henley-on-Thames," says Helen, recalling her previous home. What began with "itchy feet and a germ of an idea" resulted in Helen, husband Nick and three children moving to the sunny south west of France. They rented a house, settled the children into French schools and began the search for a home. They found the Château de Claribès, a grand 15th-century house with eleven hectares of Bordeaux vines and a winery, set amongst 25 hectares of fields and woodlands.

After taking over the estate in 2004 they began restructuring the vineyards, installing additional equipment, coping with the variable weather, and bringing in their first vintage. "It was hectic and the vats were installed the day before the harvest began," recalls Nick.

The newly renovated holiday house is next door. From a morning-sunny courtyard you enter a light open room with a contemporary kitchen, dining area and living room. The furnishings are a blend of antique and modern, the colours are muted and restful, the feeling is luxurious but inviting. A door from the kitchen leads to an outside dining area and a south west-facing enclosed garden. Up a central, open staircase are two big double rooms with windows looking out over the valley. Each bedroom contains a day bed, allowing flexible sleeping for families. And, with wood-burning stoves (the logs supplied from the

WINES

Château de Claribès, Sauvignon Blanc

A 100% sauvignon blanc, a rosé and two reds are produced here and they have won prestigious awards. The sauvignon is hand-picked in the early morning to capture the fresh aromas and fruit flavours. Dry and crisp with hints of peach, grapefruit, elderflower and vanilla, it is perfect for oysters or a mushroom and truffle oil risotto.

Wines €4.50–€15

Nick Kinder & Helen Kelly
Château de Claribès,
Claribès, 33890 Gensac
- Rooms: 1 gîte for 4, from €700 per week. Extra beds for children.
- Meals: Dinner from €25.
- Closed: Rarely.
- +33 (0)5 57 47 16 62
- www.claribes.com

estate) in both the living and the dining room, the house is super-warm and cosy: perfect for a holiday any time of year.

Salmon and trout swim up the river to spawn; Nick can arrange a fishing permit. Forage for mushrooms or explore the limestone caves, take one of the vineyard walks, follow an off-road bike trail, or relax and enjoy the tranquillity. Tours of the vineyard are welcomed and Nick will treat you to an informal tasting in the shady, open-sided tasting room.

Biodynamic techniques and organic fertilisers combine to produce healthy grapes. The grapes are harvested and fermented according to variety and vineyard parcel, and, after analysing the grape sugars each day in the lead-up to harvest, picked when they are ripe. New technologies such as temperature-controlled stainless steel tanks harmonise with traditional techniques to produce high quality, award-winning wines. Friends and family rally round to help hand-pick the delicate sauvignon blanc grapes. "Although everyone enjoys the harvesting," says Nick, "the best part of the day is sitting down together for a long leisurely lunch in the shade of the trees!"

Château de Carbonneau

GIRONDE

Near Gensac, on the left bank of the Dordogne, the country lanes wind their way through a landscape of wooded hills and valley meadows. Each turn in the road brings a new view: cattle grazing in the grass, a field of flourishing vines, a distant church spire.

Not far from Gensac is Château de Carbonneau, an elegant 19th-century manor house set in two hectares of parkland and fifteen of vines. A long avenue of trees draws you to the entrance and the beautiful orangery. Wilfred's mother came here when her family moved from New Zealand in the 1930s. Half a century later he married a New Zealander, Jacquie, and, in 1992, they returned to the family home with three young children in tow. They took on the running of the wine estate, replanted the vineyards and began creating their own wines.

Mentioned in the 1900 edition of the Grand Larousse encyclopaedia, the vineyards here have long produced wines. You can taste them at the counter-topped wine press in the tasting salon, or on the balustraded terrace. Wilfred's reds and whites come from the Sainte Foy de Bordeaux appellation, a wine growing area of sandy-gravels in the valleys and limestone-clay hillsides. Carbonneau's vines grow on the limestone slopes where the predominant merlot grape produces a rich, ripe red wine. A fruity rosé and a zingy sauvignon complete the range.

When they started, Wilfred and Jacquie had little experience, very young vines and bags of enthusiasm. They've learned some hard lessons over the years yet have maintained their enthusiastic outlook. Says Wilfred: "our goal is to make the best wine we can with the natural and human resources available to us." A clutch of stars from the respected wine guide Hachette is testimony to their achievement.

There are five guest rooms here and a graceful winding staircase adorned with Maori portraits leads to four of them. Full of subtle colour and space, each has a superb view of the parkland and vineyards; the largest has a huge tiled bathroom

WINES

Château Carbonneau,
'Cuvée Margot' Sainte Foy de Bordeaux
Wilfred's small parcel of sauvignon blanc vines has just reached maturity and is producing an excellent white wine. Typical aromas of box hedge and citrus are overlayed with more exotic, sweeter fruit. No harshness on the palate but zingy enough to make a great partner for a seafood risotto.

Wines €4.60–€14

Jacquie Franc de Ferrière
Château de Carbonneau,
33890 Pessac sur Dordogne
- Rooms: 5: 2 doubles,
  3 twins/doubles, €90–€130.
- Meals: Dinner €25. Wine €8–€20.
- Closed: December-February.
- +33 (0)5 57 47 46 46
- www.chateau-carbonneau.com

and an antique roll top bath. Downstairs there's a handsome sitting room, a formal dining room, and a broad sunny terrace where dinner and breakfast are served. There's a large double here, too, named after the antique telephone fixed to the wall; open the windows onto the scented gardens and a chorus of birdsong breaks the silence. "This is a quiet, tranquil room," says Wilfred. "And the phone hasn't rung since 1912!"

A vigneronne and a keen cook, Jacquie enjoys matching the flavours, aromas and colours of her wine with food. Her dinners are visual treats as well as taste sensations, and include produce from her potager. Many guests return; convivial dinners taken on the terrace with a backdrop of late summer sunsets are a major draw.

The Dordogne river joins two historic towns – Saint-Emilion, once a place of pilgrimage, and Bergerac, a market town of half-timbered houses and cobbled streets. The lanes and squares of both busy towns are lined with restaurants. For lunch try L'Envers du Décor in Saint-Emilion, or Lou Brageirac in Bergerac.

Château Saint-Robert

GIRONDE

The gravelly flatland between the left bank of the Garonne and the forests of the Landes enclose the Graves appellation. Prior to the Revolution, the château had been a lordly estate, but during the expansive years of the 19th century it became a celebrated wine property. Today its top wine, Cuvée Poncet-Deville, is named in honour of the man who built the house and planted Saint-Robert's immaculate vineyards.

The house, two single-storey wings, and the winery buildings form a central sheltered courtyard. Herbaceous shrubs and palm trees share a sunny lawn with tall broad-leafed trees; the green herb-scented garden is filled with birdsong and doves coo on a first-floor balcony. The house has an understated elegance, with its pale stucco façade, neo-classical doorways and sun-faded shutters.

Saint-Robert is a group-owned estate so you will be greeted and hosted by a team. Jean-Claude is a knowledgeable and enthusiastic fan of this region and he can arrange tours and tastings at the group's three other Bordeaux châteaux, two on the Right Bank near Pomerol, and one in Sauternes. A half-day trip to some of these wineries will give you an insight into the rich diversity of Bordeaux's wine styles.

Bedrooms here are on the south wing's ground floor and the three restrained 'chambres au château' look out onto a tidy potager, a giant umbrella pine, and the vineyards. Antiques add a stylish gravitas and large comfortable beds are cosy with quilted, patterned spreads. "We leave a complimentary bottle of the estate's wine in each room," says Jean-Claude. "A glass makes a good pick-me-up after the drive here!" Next to the bedrooms is an impressive drawing room – a convivial place for a game of French billiards or a sociable chat by the fireside. The breakfast room is reached via a light, bright hallway which doubles as a sitting area. On warm summer mornings a breakfast

WINES

Château Saint-Robert, Graves

This unoaked Graves has a dense, brilliant colour. Harmoniously balanced on the palate, this is an elegant, fruity wine that's pleasant to drink young; the tannins, which will soften more with a little extra cellaring, bring the wine its complexity. Why not try it with rare roast beef and Yorkshire pudding?

Wines €8–€16

M Belanger
Château Saint-Robert,
33210 Pujols sur Ciron
- Rooms: 3: 2 doubles, 1 twin, €95–€110.
- Meals: Restaurant 7km.
- Closed: October-April.
- +33 (0)5 57 31 07 55
- www.chambre-saintrobert.com

of warm breads and patisseries, fresh from the village bakery, is served on a tree-shaded patio at the edge of the vineyard.

Wine tastings happen in the vaulted cellars beneath the house; the reds and whites are both made with hand-picked grapes that are also sorted by hand and then matured in stainless steel vats. Some wines are fruity and approachable and the oak aged Cuvée Poncet-Deville wines are complex and structured and will age well.

Thirty-four hectares of vines surround the house – walk to the edge and you find a vast forest within which are hidden chapels, ruined windmills and Romanesque churches. Hire bikes nearby and explore the Graves area along a number of well-marked cycle paths that are mostly on the flat. From the village of Cérons there's a frequent and fast train service to Bordeaux, the epicentre of this world-famous wine region. By car you can explore the vine lands that follow the Garonne river as far as Toulouse, or head west to the wild Atlantic coast.

La Maison des Vignes

GIRONDE

Sometimes life's most significant decisions begin as a frivolous dream. So it was for Pascal Méli when he spotted the details for 'a winemaker's property of 15 hectares' near Bourg-en-Gironde. "I never imagined buying such an amazing place but I thought, 'why not take a look?'" Within six months, he and his wife Marielle had moved into Château Bujan and were celebrating their first grape harvest. Pascal beams: "The following year we received gold and silver medals for our first ever vintage, the 1987."

Twenty-two harvests later and Bujan is still home to Pascal, Marielle and their three children. Originally from Paris, they had never intended to become winemakers; Marielle studied architecture and still has her own practice; Pascal was an agricultural consultant in Normandy. Neither comes from a winemaking family but they overcame the daily challenges of their new life with hard work and a big dose of luck. "We were blessed with good friends whose morale-boosting and financial support helped us through the early years."

Since then, in spite of the endless cycle of pruning, growing, harvesting and winemaking, the Méli family found the time and resources to restore the beautiful Maison des Vignes: a 17th-century house, overlooking the vine-strewn valley. Marielle's flair for design has resulted in a harmonious blend of old and new. In your kitchen-salon, chunky cream painted beams and muted earth-coloured walls give a stylish and natural feel.

Anything with a plug (including the kitchen sink) is discreetly hidden within the large oak dresser, painted the palest grey-blue. There's a serious oven and a battery of heavy pans. Dine elegantly at the pine table that seats up to eight guests, then flop on big comfy sofas by the stone fireplace. Next door are two double bedrooms decorated in the same subtle hues, sharing a large bathroom with a magnificent claw-foot bath; upstairs are two more bedrooms.. A rustic summer 'dining room' at the back of the house is perfect for barbecues; beyond is the pool and gardens.

WINES

Château Bujan, Côtes de Bourg

Merlot and cabernet vines grown on limestone and clay soils produce these rich and aromatic Côtes de Bourgs. Each harvest puts its stamp on the wine's personality but all Pascal's vintages share a core of ripe black fruit in harmony with toasty oak. Broach a bottle an hour or so before serving pan-fried duck breast with a blackcurrant sauce.
Wines €5.70–€15

Pascal & Marielle Méli
La Maison des Vignes,
Château Bujan, 33710 Gauriac
• Rooms: Gîte for 8,
  €950–€1,900 per week.
• Meals: Restaurant 2km.
• Closed: Rarely.
• +33 (0)5 57 64 86 56
• www.chateau-bujan.com

"We have five different grape varieties: merlot, cabernet sauvignon, cabernet franc, malbec and petit verdot," explains Pascal. "The climate and soil has a different effect on each and creates specific characteristics." To exploit these to the full, the vines are grown separately in agricultural sections known as 'parcelles'. Each parcelle's grapes are harvested as they reach optimum ripeness, then fermented in separate vats. "In the springtime the wines are blended – et voilà, the wine is born!" says Pascal.

The Bujan wines are elegant, complex and balanced. The Mélis have received many accolades including a Decanter World Wine award in 2006. Pascal's vines benefit from near-perfect conditions and he is careful not to disrupt nature's balance. Chemical insecticides are banned; where possible, he ploughs between the rows and does not use herbicides. "We're not blind to scientific knowledge, but we love to experiment, and to innovate." In certain years, Pascal makes a particular cuvée, Les Copains (the friends). Many who've stayed here over the years would be happy to be counted among them.

Peyraguey Maison Rouge

GIRONDE

The Sauternais, forty kilometres south of Bordeaux, is made up of a patchwork of low-lying vineyards and delicious pale stone properties ranging from small farms to grand châteaux. Its rare sweet wine made it famous and the best examples come from a handful of 'first growth' properties between Sauternes and Barsac. In the centre of the region, surrounded by premier cru classé vineyards, is the family home of Annick and Jean-Claude Belanger.

Peyraguey Maison Rouge is a charming 19th-century longère with three elegant guest rooms. From the patio you get a privileged view of Château d'Yquem, whose wine, said Thomas Jefferson, was "the best of all Sauternes". At the bottom of the garden a herd of Bazadaise cows graze between the trees and the priceless vines – a mere stroll away.

Annick relates the history of their 'petite maison'. "The house was originally a row of cottages built for the vineyard workers. It was rendered in red stucco and became known as The Red House. It was in a terrible state when we arrived in 2002, and the renovations took a year." Now, above the wine cellar, up a covered flight of steps, is the biggest of the chambres d'hôtes. Médoc is a light room whose windows give a broad view of the fortified château of Lafaurie and the banks of the Garonne. Antique furniture, seagrass matting and beautiful colours make this a refined and inviting room.

In the main house are two rooms on the ground floor. The warmly elegant Saint Emilion opens onto the courtyard and at dusk the windows reveal the westering sun. Sauternes, on the eastern side, opens to the gardens and the pool. Beamed ceilings and Gironde tiled floors are authentically rustic; bathrooms are the best of contemporary. Next door is the guests' sitting room, a charming room with a Girondine fireplace in pale stone.

WINES

Château Destanque Sauternes

Château Destanque, from the best terroirs of Barsac, is one of the smallest Sauternes properties. Two hectares of vines near the river Ciron produce a wine with a fine bouquet of pear, with a touch of honey and a delicious, juicy palate. Traditionally served with foie gras, it should also be tried with the grapey roast quail dish, Cailles aux Raisins.

Wines from €15

M Belanger
Peyraguey Maison Rouge,
Bommes, 33210 Sauternes
- Rooms: 3: 2 doubles, 1 twin, €72–€90.
- Meals: Restaurants 2km.
- Closed: Rarely.
- +33 (0)5 57 31 07 55
- www.peyraguey-sauternes.com

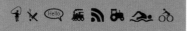

Jean-Claude is a négotiant (a broker who buys direct from the vineyards) and has no commercial vineyards. He does, however, have a small patch of vines in front of the house. As it's just outside the area classified as Sauternes, the wine is reserved for family and friends. "If this vineyard had the same status as those a few metres away, the wine would be worth a small fortune!" he says.

As a 'négoce', he keeps a range of wines and a tasting here will include dry Graves as well as Sauternes. Sauternes, a wine that needs hot summers and sunny autumns, also requires a special ingredient, 'la pourriture noble'. Jean-Claude explains the benefits of this 'noble rot'. "Early morning mists from the rivers Garonne and Ciron settle in the vineyards and bring with them the spores of the botrytis fungus. The microbe attacks the skins of the ripe fruit and the water inside each grape starts to evaporate. In hot years, when la pourriture works its magic, sugar levels in the fruit are super concentrated, and so the wine attains its honeyed sweetness."

Château Lavanau
LOT-ET-GARONNE

Paul Uhart has France and farming in his blood. His French father moved to England from the Basque country during the Second World War. "I was born and raised on the family's farm in East Anglia, but knew one day I would return to France." Paul and his artist wife Juliana came to the Duras hills via Paris, where they lived and worked for fifteen years.

Château Lavanau sits between the great wine rivers of the Dordogne and the Garonne, in the Côtes de Duras region. You approach the pale apricot house along a short driveway between the plum trees and a pretty garden whose pond is alive with a chorus of amorous frogs. The blue-shuttered windows may be typically French but the scene on the croquet lawn, as a game comes to an end, is very British. You are welcomed with a cup of English tea or a glass of Paul's excellent wine.

Plum orchards and vineyards surround the property and Paul produces 'pruneaux d'Agen' from

his trees as well as Côtes de Duras wines. Juliana, whose artistic talents transformed the farmhouse into a beautiful chambres d'hotes, teaches art in a studio overlooking the winery.

There are five light, bright and welcoming rooms, three upstairs and one on the ground floor, opening to the morning-sunny terrace. Breakfast (try the prunes!) is served in a bright dining room that once guarded the wine vats, or on a terrace by the pool. For other meals there's a guest kitchen.

Juliana studied at St Martin's School of Art in London and her work has been shown in galleries all over Europe. She worked as a teacher and her enthusiasm and guidance have released hidden talents in the most unpromising students. "I provide the easels and encouragement," she says, modestly, "but my students do the rest, here in the studio or out in the fields." Lessons in

WINES

**Château Lavanau,
Côtes de Duras**

Is it Paul's bounteous plum orchards that give his wine such a ripe plummy bouquet? Other fruits are there too – sometimes cherry and bilberry – depending on the vintage. A smooth but concentrated palate expresses the fruit without any harshness and you can drink it from its third year. The perfect match for a spicy North African lamb tagine cooked with prunes, 'pruneaux d'Agen'. **Wines from €4**

Juliana & Paul Uhart
Château Lavanau,
Les Faux, 47120 Loubès Bernac
- Rooms: 5: 3 doubles, 2 twins,
  €65–€75.
- Meals: Restaurant 1km. Guest kitchen.
- Closed: Rarely.
- +33 (0)5 53 94 86 45
- www.chateaulavanau.com

drawing, watercolours, acrylics and oils are available for groups of up to twelve, or as private sessions.

Across the courtyard is the tidy winery where Paul produces his distinctive wines. These wines were highly regarded during the reign of Louis XIV – so much so that the Sun King's mistress planned the death of the abbot who controlled the lands to secure the vineyards for herself. "When we say that Duras wines are to die for, it's historically true!"

Paul has invested in modern temperature controlled vats to produce wine from the seven hectares of vines on the highest south-facing limestone slopes, known as the 'cradle of Duras'. He maintains his wines should never try to emulate Bordeaux but be celebrated for their own distinctiveness. His skill has been praised in England and in France.

Grapes from the twenty-year-old vines are picked by machine at the peak of their ripeness and brought inside during the cool of the evening to help them maintain their plumpness. "Just as chefs need to work with the freshest ingredients," says Paul, "a winemaker needs grapes at the peak of freshness."

Château Haut Garrigue

DORDOGNE

The genius of wine is nature. Without the magical force that "through the green fuse drives the flower" there would be no grapes and, without grapes, no wine. Caroline and Sean Feely understand that nature is everything when it comes to wine-making and they cultivate their organic vineyard bio-dynamically.

Ancestral links to the wine trade and a passion for France inspired the Feelys. Sean's father was raised on a Cape wine farm and a branch of Caroline's family were 18th-century 'wine geese' – wealthy Irish traders who established some famous Bordeaux châteaux. "The names of several top estates still have a familiar Irish ring," says Caroline: Lynch-Bages, Kirwan, Leoville-Barton, Phelan-Ségur. The couple met in South Africa, then followed city careers in Dublin before moving to this hilltop farm near the village of Saussignac in 2005.

The farmhouse has a long association with the vine: etched into the wall of the winery is the date 1737 and parts of the cellars are much, much older. The view of the vineyards from the dapple-shady patio has changed little over the centuries. In the apartment (called 'The Grape Escape') you go straight into a large modern kitchen and dining area. To the side is the grand salon: a big, bright room with windows on three sides to drink in the wonderful view, deep sofas and an inglenook. Stay here for a week and take part in wine workshops; you can rent a row of vines, too, and get involved in every aspect of viticultural life.

Sean's ten hectares of Bergerac vines ("just enough for the family to manage") cling to steep limestone and clay slopes. Not far from the left bank of the Dordogne, the soil, climate and position are perfectly suited for making the delicious sweet wine Saussignac; they make good dry white, red and strawberry-fruity rosés here too.

But what of biodynamics? This holistic farming system, synchronised with the lunar calendar, guides every aspect of the work – from pruning and harvesting in the vineyard, to

WINES

Château Haut Garrigue, Saussignac

Hand-picked fruit, low yields and nature's magic deliver a heavenly, golden wine. You'll find honey and passionfruit in the glass with hints of almond, honeysuckle and orange blossom. Open a bottle to have with a starter of terrine de foie gras and save a little for the dessert – an apricot tarte tatin would be perfect.

Wines €5.99–€15

stirring the lees and bottling in the cellars. Homeopathic preparations add an extra boost to the health of the vines and the soil: nettle tea is used as a tonic, willow as a curative, horsetail as a natural fungicide. Sceptical at first, Caroline became a convert to biodynamism when she witnessed the results. "Rare orchids began to flourish in the fields, wild garlic and fennel sprouted between the vine rows, and the birds and the beasts came back. Such a rich biodiversity means that destructive pests are kept in check by natural predators, and the healthier, stronger plants can resist disease. Next we began to see the positive changes to the fruit – yields have been reduced, but the quality of the wine has soared." It has won many awards, too.

It's a short walk to Saussignac to buy your daily bread, market day is Friday and there's a good restaurant in the village, too. In fact, you could spend days here without using the car – a cycle ride along the 'grand randonée', a stroll in the woods and vineyards in search of wild birds or wild mushrooms, a lazy afternoon's reading beneath a shady fig.

Seán & Caroline Feely
Château Haut Garrigue,
24240 Saussignac
- Rooms: 1 twin/double, €75.
  Gîte for 4, €295–€550 per week.
- Meals: Breakfast €5. Restaurant 850m.
  Picnics available.
- Closed: No B&B from June-September.
- +33 (0)5 53 22 72 71
- www.hautgarrigue.com

Château Les Farcies Du Pech'

DORDOGNE

Bergerac's steep cobbled lanes lead from the old bridge by the quayside to a town square bursting with the colours, sounds and smells of the market: the farmers set up shop on Wednesday and Saturday mornings. On the hillsides, a mile of so from this lovely atmospheric town, are the vines.

During centuries of trading with England and the Low Countries, certain vineyards gained a reputation for exceptional quality. One such is Pécharmant – the 'charming hill'. It is still regarded as one of the best and you can discover its wines at Château Les Farcies du Pech'. This is a family-run estate owned by local winemaker Serge Dubard; his sister-in-law Marie manages the beautiful chambres d'hôtes, his brother cultivates the vines. The family arrived during the great storm of 1999, and made their first vintage following the perfect harvest of 2000.

Rebuilt during the Napoleonic Empire, this elegantly proportioned 'chartreuse' – or

Perigordian house – has vestiges of a château built in the 1600s. On one side, the house and winery form a sheltered courtyard; on the other, the shuttered façade surveys eight hectares of parkland. A skilful restoration on the interior has conserved the fabric and character of the building. Oak posts and beams and herringbone brickwork are joyfully exposed, as are the ancient tiles on the ground floor and the original floorboards upstairs. Paintings, engravings and objets d'art decorate the walls; in the hallway, at the foot of a beautiful oak staircase, a statuette of Cyrano de Bergerac delivers a soliloquy to new arrivals.

There are five big double rooms, two on the ground floor and three upstairs. The restrained and elegant décor adds to the rooms' charm, while the Empire-style chairs, armoires and fireplaces evoke the house's 19th-century heyday. The farmhouse

WINES

Château Les Farcies du Pech', Pécharmant

The charming hill of Pécharmant certainly produces a charming wine. The flattering mix of ripe black fruit and subtle oak will seduce even the most stalwart claret fans. Delicious on its own, try it with a Landaise salad for starters or noisettes of lamb with a black truffle Perigourdine sauce.

Wines €6.50–€8.50

2005
PÉCHARMANT
APPELLATION PÉCHARMANT CONTRÔLÉE

Serge Dubard
Château Les Farcies Du Pech',
Les Farcies, 24100 Bergerac
• Rooms: 5 doubles, from €100.
• Meals: Restaurants in town.
• Closed: November-March.
• +33 (0)5 53 82 48 31
• www.vignoblesdubard.com

kitchen with its huge fireplace and open studwork is unusually handsome. You are welcome to use the kitchen to prepare a simple meal; for larger groups Marie lays on a vigneron's feast that includes such rich local delicacies as goose rillettes and confit de canard.

Serge has ten hectares of cabernet and merlot vines on the south-facing, sand-gravel slopes of Pécharmant. The geology and the mix of grape varieties make these wines closer in character to the wines of the Médoc than to those of the neighbouring Côtes de Bordeaux. As Serge explains, "we have an equal mix of cabernet sauvignon, cabernet franc and merlot in the blend and, all being well, we make a well-structured wine with an aromatic character."

The river Dordogne, that once carried Bergerac wine to the ports of Bordeaux and Royan, has become a haven for wildlife. It also draws water-loving holidaymakers: canoes and kayaks can be hired upstream. Spot a wily otter, glimpse the iridescent flash of a kingfisher as you paddle the river's gentle, expansive waters.

Domaine de Lauroux

GERS

Nick and Karen found the vineyard of their dreams in the rolling hills of the Gers in Gascony. Domaine de Lauroux was their antidote to stress-filled, corporate life: no pollution, no motorways, the land providing almost all you need. They moved here in 2004, spruced-up the winery and learned the secrets of viticulture. The winery is unique: as far as Nick knows, he's the only Englishman in the world distilling Gascon brandy, Armagnac. He makes excellent wines, too.

The house and winery are set in 40 hectares of vines, pasture and woods and before Nick and Karen arrived, Lauroux had been farmed by several generations of the same Gascon family. "The estate is intact, just as it was in the 1800s," says Nick, "so the vineyards are all in one block." The view over the serried rows, framed by orchards and woodland, hasn't changed during two centuries.

The Kitcheners created a cosy gîte in an old vine workers' cottage and a smart studio in the main house. La Petite, the cottage, has been sympathetically converted... original wooden floors upstairs, a beamed ceiling in the kitchen and homely hearths. In the three bedrooms, cast-iron bedsteads and Karen's collection of country furniture go well with the simple, white décor. Cooking is a pleasure in the well-equipped kitchen and there's a super barbecue cheminée on the veranda. The gardens, perfumed with lavender, laurel and fruit tree blossom, lead to the private terrace of the studio. Indoors there are original fireplaces, wonderful Italian marble floors and authentic country furniture.

Breakfasts are a treat: homemade jams (try the fig and Armagnac), fruit from the orchard and Karen's almond and apricot muffins made with Lauroux's free-range eggs. Karen loves to cook the hearty French country food for which Gascony is famous. Enjoy a fabulous evening meal and reflect,

contentedly, on the Gascon paradox – that the people of this region cook exclusively with duck or goose fat, and yet have the lowest levels of heart disease in the world.

Gascony's wines are honest, authentic and tasty. Nick swears by his adage that "good grapes make good wine" and, to produce both, he uses biodynamically-approved treatments coupled with a hands-on approach in the vineyard. "But," he explains, "in the winery we intervene very little, allowing natural yeasts to ferment the grapes, and keeping sulphites to an absolute minimum. Animal by-products are banned so Lauroux wines are suitable for vegetarians and vegans."

Nick's wines have been praised by the British press and have even received friendly and flattering reviews from France's Guide Hachette. You can taste and buy 'at the cellar door' in the purpose-built tasting room. Choose from the sweet, dry, red, white and rosé wines; Floc de Gascogne (the region's fortified aperitif); and the amber-hued Bas-Armagnac spirits. Of these last, Nick has vintages going back to 1929.

WINES

**Domaine de Lauroux,
Bas-Armagnac Côtes de Gascogne**
Look at its bright colour, warm it in the hollow of your hand and enjoy the bouquet of fruit, flowers, spices and that elusive nutty aroma known as 'rancio'. Finally, sip it slowly to appreciate its strength, smoothness and rich aromatic flavour. Have a small glass with your morning coffee or with a slice of walnut and Armagnac tarte.
Wines €3.75–€5.50;
Armagnac €9–€750

Karen Kitchener
Domaine de Lauroux, 32370 Manciet
• Rooms: Studio double from €70.
  Gîte for 6, €500–€1,100 per week.
• Meals: Dinner with wine, €20.
  Restaurant 2km.
• Closed: Rarely.
• +33 (0)5 62 08 56 76
• www.lauroux.com

LANGUEDOC – ROUSSILLON

LANGUEDOC – ROUSSILLON

France's largest wine region follows the Mediterranean coast from the Pyrenees to the Rhône delta. The Languedoc, with its southern neighbour the Roussillon, share a mountainous landscape where fortified hilltop towns and abbey ruins survey a vast area of vines. Along a coastline of long sandy beaches and brackish lakes, the fishing villages and the smaller seaside resorts have an undeveloped charm; mass tourism has not yet tamed this wild country of bull-fighting and rugby football. Its dynamic, pioneering winemakers have earned the region the title, 'France's New World'.

From antiquity, vines have played an important role in the Languedoc economy and Narbonne, once the capital of the Roman province of Narbonensis, is still the centre-point of its vine lands. To the south of the city are the Corbières vineyards; Limoux, with its sparkling wines; and the sweet-wine areas of Banyuls, Rivesaltes and Maury – France's southernmost vineyards. North of Narbonne, the Coteaux du Languedoc follow the coastline through Bezier and Montpellier. On higher ground, further inland, are the vineyards of the Minervois, Saint Chinian and Faugères. A third of all French wine is made here and, in recent years, the region has begun to build a reputation for the quality as well as the quantity of its production.

The Languedoc's food is varied, flavoursome and healthy. The locals understand that few of life's pleasures surpass a simple, tasty dinner shared between friends. Olive oil, fresh fish and seafood are available in abundance in the coastal regions; goat's cheese, lamb, and wild game, like boar and hare, are found in the hinterland where there's very little dairy farming. Many of the region's specialities are associated with particular towns: Carcassonne's cassoulet, a hearty casserole of beans, confited goose and pork; Sète's fishy stew, bourride; and oysters and mussels from Bouzigues. Culinary influences from Spain and North Africa have brought paella, tapas and tajine to the region's cafés and restaurants.

The Languedoc has a distinctive accent and its own language after which it was named. The langue d'oc (the oc language) is making a comeback, as is a pride in being Occitan. The Catalan language, a close relative of Occitan, is spoken by many in the Roussillon.

The medieval Cathar heretics were bloodily suppressed in the Albigensian crusade and in 1702 the protestant Huguenots were driven to civil war in the Cévennes hills. The Cathars are long gone but many of their 13th-century castles and strongholds still stand. Earlier relics, too, have survived intact like Le Pont du Gard (the Roman aqueduct shown opposite), the amphitheatre at Nîmes and several stretches of the Roman road, the Via Domitia.

Each of the properties in this section has a fascinating story to tell and, as you might expect in this New World of French wine, their owners are an international bunch. You can stay at a grand château or a fortified bastide, a traditional mas farmhouse or an ultra-modern winery. Join in the grape harvest at one; gain a professional wine qualification in another. Mourvèdre, the traditional local grape, is said only to ripen in vineyards overlooking the sea; and it's the Mediterranean of course that creates the region's warm, sunny climate.

Domaine Gayda
LANGUEDOC - ROUSSILLON

On the Languedoc plains, below the foothills of the Pyrenees, is a very special domaine. During three frenetic years, Tim Ford and his talented team transformed a field of sunflowers into a productive vineyard, built an amazing ultra-modern winery, and created an award-wining wine. Next came a fine-dining restaurant, a clutch of beautifully converted holiday cottages, and the launch of an international wine school. Domaine Gayda is one of the latest (and hottest) properties on the dynamic and ever-changing Languedoc wine scene; you won't find it on the map and your GPS might not recognise the name!

How was it that this English horticulturist came to realise such an ambitious project? The life-size bronze of a crouching cheetah gives you a clue. In 2002 Tim met Anthony Record, a South African born businessman and MBE. "Our shared love of the Languedoc, its wild beauty and its

wines, led us to buy the land here," Tim explains. "Then, on a fact-finding tour of the Cape winelands, we met Vincent Chansault, a young French œnologue, who came back with us to help design, build and equip the new winery."

The team also includes one of South Africa's top winemakers, an English Master of Wine and a celebrated Belgian chef. Between them they have created more than bricks and mortar, vine rows and vat houses. Since the first vintage of 2005 Gayda has won high scores from Wine Spectator and Decanter, and journalists like Steven Spurrier and Jancis Robinson are fans.

A visit to the state-of-the-art winery will reveal how the estate's wines are made. Tim explains that their methods owe much to the South African way of winemaking: "We combine the grapes from our own vineyards here and in the Minervois with those of our partner vine growers

from some of the best vineyards in the region. Having such a rich palate of fruit from several different soils, grape varieties and microclimates allows us to make a range of wines." The range includes fruity single varieties, harmonious blends, innovative and experimental cuvées and true 'terroir' wines.

Gayda's young vines cover ten hectares of gently sloping fields near the village of Brugairolles between Carcassonne and Limoux. The winery is an impressive building on two high floors. Stone arches and sheets of glass punctuate the pale-golden façade and support a low-pitched roof of sun-faded terracotta tiles.

The serious work of turning grapes into wine goes on in the cellars below; upstairs are the offices and the smart, contemporary restaurant with stunningly scenic views of the Pyrenees and the all-encompassing vines.

The dining area continues onto a covered terrace and into the herb-scented gardens where you encounter a group of straw-capped wooden huts ('paillotes' in French, 'rondevals' in Afrikaans). Here you can dine, safari-style, to the accompaniment of singing crickets, if not roaring lions. Pascal Ledroit is the chef, a Belgian cuisinier who worked in many star-rated establishments and ran his own acclaimed restaurants in Melbourne and Brussels. His love for this wild region and his passion for Mediterranean food brought him to Gayda. The creative, modern cuisine is a delight – try a glass of the estate's viognier with a fillet of seared salmon, rocket-flavoured butter and spicy, red Marseillette rice.

If a taste of the wines here inspires you to learn more about the Languedoc Roussillon then why not enrol at the wine school? Called Vinécole, the school is based at the Gayda winery and residential course-

goers get to stay in the oh-so-smart guest cottages within the grounds. A day's tuition or just a couple of hours of discovery are available for starters; more serious students can even take their professional exams here. Matthew Stubbs, the English Master of Wine and Emma Kershaw lead the courses which, although thoroughly professional, are designed to be fun. Emma explains that a hands-on, nose-in approach is the best way to learn, "The subtleties of wine can't be learned from the pages of a book. Wine needs to be tasted. And when you've experienced the aromas, the flavours, even the emotions it evokes, the rest is easy." Half-day introductions to the Languedoc, an area that Matthew calls "the most exciting wine region in the world", are great for beginners; a full day's pruning, blending and tasting gives you a real feel for the

"The subtleties of wine can't be learned from the pages of a book. Wine needs to be tasted. When you have experienced the aromas and the flavours, the rest is easy"

vigneron's work. Themed Master Classes cover a range of topics from biodynamics to the sticky subject of matching sweet wines with chocolate!

Gayda is not all about learning though. Down a private road through the vineyards, four delightful cottages provide accommodation for wine students and holidaymakers. Thoughtfully restored and converted, the houses create a U-shaped courtyard shaded by mature trees and perfumed by the aromatic herbs that border the lawns.

Comfort and modernity blend satisfyingly in the resplendent interiors and echoes of the rural past (exposed stone walls, wood-burning stoves and ancient beamed ceilings) form a natural backdrop for the rich soft furnishings,

WINES

Domaine Gayda, 'Chemin de Moscou' Vin de Pays d'Oc
In the village of Brugairolles, old terraced vines from the vineyard called 'The Road to Moscow' produce a deep purple wine with a spicy bouquet of violet, cinnamon and hedgerow fruits. Already complex in its third year, this wine will continue to improve. Try a bottle with 'pigeonneau du Lauragais', pigeon roasted with salsify and parsnips.
Wines from €4.15

original paintings and African pottery. In the living rooms, deep sofas and antique kilims sit on tiled or polished oak floors; the kitchens, either clean-line contemporary or classic country-style, are immaculate and well equipped. The light, bright, stylish bedrooms are spacious; some are huge. Spotless bathrooms have super walk-in showers, all mod cons and great lighting.

Each cottage has its own private area of the courtyard and, for sociable encounters there's an impressive bar/games room, a huge kitchen and indoor dining area plus a pool-side barbecue room in a converted barn. There are two pristine pools (one for young children, the other for the young at heart) and a new tennis court, all with wonderful views of the distant hills that await discovery.

Up to twenty guests can stay here and from Easter to September the cottages tend to be booked en-bloc for corporate groups. Out of season you can rent one of the houses for a week's holiday or even (Carcassonne airport is only a half-hour drive) a weekend.

Emma Kershaw
Domaine Gayda, Chemin de Moscou, 11300 Brugairolles

- Rooms: 3 gîtes for 4, 1 gîte for 8, from €700 per week. Whole property from €3,750 per week.
- Meals: Lunch from €21.95; dinner with wine from €39.
- Closed: Never.
- +33 (0)4 68 31 64 14
- www.domainegayda.com

Château La Villatade

AUDE

Villatade is a traditional 'campagne': a closed-courtyard farmhouse that, in its heyday, housed a self-sufficient community living off the land. Today only your hosts live here but, as Denis explains, "when our guests arrive the house comes alive with friendly conversation and bonhomie." The atmosphere is infectious – visitors who drop in for a quick wine tasting often lose track of the time.

Denis and Sophie Morin had always been fond of the Minervois. So when they decided to forego their careers and make a new start, their quest began here, between Carcassonne and the Black Mountain. What they discovered was Château la Villatade, an ancient Languedocian farm with twenty-two hectares of vineyards and a square kilometre of pine forest and wild garrigue. They restored the house, became winemakers and have lived and worked in their "corner of paradise" for over fifteen years.

A couple of hikers who arrived looking for a bed one night inspired Sophie to name their ground-floor suite The Walkers' Suite. No backpacker's bedroom, it's a stunning little bolthole for two plus kitchenette – charming, comfortable and contemporary. For larger groups, or for those who wish to stay a week or more, there are two self-catering options. Once a barn with a hayloft above, Wine Cottage is a beautiful split-level conversion with high beamed ceilings, terracotta floors and lime-washed walls. There are two double bedrooms and a bunkroom for kids. You can relax in the large light living room or on the small shady terrace, your meals accompanied by views. Within the thick stone walls of Villatade itself is Courtyard Cottage, a rustic-chic house on two floors with three double rooms and a children's bedroom. Both cottages have an open fireplace and Denis and Sophie make sure that you have a supply of logs.

There are horses in the paddock, a potager and a well-stocked trout pond. You can explore the untamed wilderness

or stroll among the well-trained vines; from winter to the harvest the arduous cycle of pruning, turning the soil and fertilising (with organic manure) maintains an immaculate vineyard. A diverse mix of red Languedoc grape varieties includes one of the very few grapes to bear red juice – a Spanish varietal called alicante.

To taste the wines you step inside a novel tasting room, an enormous 19th-century wine vat where, in times past, hundreds of hectolitres of grapes were turned into wine. Denis's wines have an aromatic complexity that Sophie says comes from the natural world. "We breathe in the aromas in the vineyard; in the winery we strive to capture them for the glass." Beyond the courtyard and the chestnut-shady grounds are breathtaking mountain-top panoramas, caves and gorges. Nearby, too, is the finest fortified medieval city in Europe, Carcassonne. And Lastours, once a stronghold of the besieged Cathars. In the village below is a restaurant whose star-rated chef is a friend of the Morins; do visit if you can.

WINES

**Château la Villatade,
'Le Rituel' Minervois**
Denis strives to extract the fruit, spice and herbal qualities of the syrah grape whilst controlling its power and tannins. The results of attentive work, Le Rituel has a complex and spicy bouquet of black fruit and wild thyme. The generous, structured palate is neither too weighty nor too firm. For this wild wine, try a civet (stew) of wild boar served with olive bread and roasted vegetables.
Wines €5–€12.50

Sophie & Denis Morin
Château La Villatade,
La Villatade, 11600 Sallèles Cabardès
• Rooms: 3 twins/doubles,
  €60–€80 (one with kitchen).
  2 gîtes for 2-9, from €400 per week.
• Meals: Dinner €15.
• Closed: January.
• +33 (0)4 68 77 57 51
• www.villatade.com

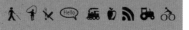

Domaine Metairie Neuve

AUDE

The Minervois is a landscape of limestone hills capped with forests of oak and Aleppo pine. Myriad tracks link its small farms and villages and bring walkers in search of wildlife, grand vistas and the fascinating history of the land of the Cathars.

A few miles to the northeast of the medieval city of Carcassonne and far from its tourist crowds is this small farm: La Metairie Neuve owned by the Boyer family who grow grapes and olives on the high south-facing slopes above the village of Laure Minervois. Marie-Hélène Boyer has lived here since 1958 and today her two sons François and Pierre run the wine business. François grows the grapes, his brother is the winemaker.

The eighty-two hectares of land once produced a huge quantity of vin ordinaire that was sold in bulk to a wholesaler. Nowadays the brothers have reduced yields, use only organic fertilisers and concentrate on making modern, varietal wines. As François explains: "We now aim for quality, not quantity, and make wines from single grape varieties like merlot and syrah. We have responded to consumer trends."

The wines win many awards but fewer than 10,000 bottles are produced. None of the wine is exported, so you really should take some home with you. With the days of large-scale production long gone, they had no choice but to diversify into bed and breakfast, as many winemaking families have.

To that end, they have restored an old stone house with white shutters and sun-faded tiles and made a rather wonderful chambres d'hôtes: Le Sol. There is a large, light bedroom with tiled floors, pale plaster walls, a high beamed ceiling and a modern shower room. Breakfast on the lawn amid camellias and singing crickets – with luck, you may be joined by Bob, a very friendly English Setter.

The true beauty of this place is unveiled with even the gentlest exploration of the surrounding countryside. Leave the car and walk through the vineyards and woods along miles of footpaths; you might chance upon a megalithic burial chamber or the remains of a 9th-century Visigothic church; Gothic finds from the church are on display at the local museum. For less active explorers, the wooded gardens next to the winery make for an idle afternoon – take a picnic and just flop in the sun.

Carcassonne is a short distance away and well worth the trip; the present-day fortifications were reconstructed in the 19th-century but the ramparts date from the Gallo-Roman period. Come to discover the town's somewhat gruesome history and learn about its role in the Albigensian Crusades and the Hundred Years' War. If history's not your thing, you could wander to a local brasserie and tuck into the rich, bean stew for which Carcassonne is famous – cassoulet. Don't leave without sampling the wine (as if) back at the domaine: Marie-Hélène offers tasting sessions in the old forge to all her visitors.

WINES

Domaine Metairie Neuve, 'Incarnat' Minervois
Incarnat means 'crimson' and it's the name of the local red marble nearby. The wine, made with merlot grapes, is also a crimson colour. The western vineyards are midway between two climate zones (Atlantic and Mediterranean) and the wine's aroma has a Bordeaux edge and a blackcurrant fruit and a rustic finish. Try with cassoulet or navarin of lamb.

Wines €3.50-€5.50

Marie-Hélène Boyer
Domaine Metairie Neuve,
11800 Laure-Minervois
- Rooms: 1 twin/double, €50-€60.
- Meals: Restaurant 5km.
- Closed: Rarely.
- +33 (0)4 68 78 00 78

Château Haute-Fontaine

AUDE

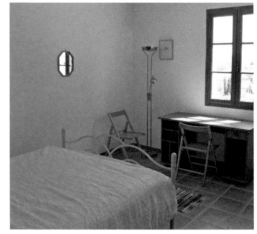

Near Narbonne, on the ancient road the Romans called the Via Domitia, is the little village of Prat de Cest. Hanibal and his elephants came past here in the 3rd century BC and the place name recalls over two millennia of history. Prat de Cest derives from the Latin for 'six leagues past' because the village is eighteen miles (or six Roman leagues) from the next staging post in Fitou. A mile-long avenue off the Roman road leads to Château Haute Fontaine, the home of English winemakers Paul and Penelope Dudson.

Geologists by training, Paul went into finance and Penny became a music teacher. By the time the children left home they were ready for a new challenge and decided to buy a wine property. The decision wasn't taken lightly, as Penny explains, "We agonised over the purchase and settled on a lucky dip: we wrote 'yes' on two pieces of paper and 'no' on another two and each had one pick. Thankfully we both picked a 'yes' and we moved in 2007."

There was a large farm here in the 13th century when these lands formed part of the estate of the abbey of Fontfroide. A well-travelled engineer built the present house in the 18th century; his journeys to the Far East inspired the colourful Javanese roof tiles and the decorative pagodas. From the landscaped lawns the façade resembles that of a grand Bordeaux château. But in the south wing, the old stable yard has a more Burgundian feel. It's a house with several faces and many surprises: there's a chapel, an ancient dovecote and the ruins of a windmill in the vines.

Called Java, the gîte has a balconied terrace and a sunny pool on the high, south-facing ridge. From here the views of the Étang de Bages on the Mediterranean coast and the distant peaks of the Pyrenees are almost Tuscan. There's a well-equipped, modern kitchen, and through a door leading from the sun-blessed terrace is a large

WINES

Château Haute-Fontaine, 'Grand Réserve Corbières'
Picked by hand, the old syrah, carignan and mourvèdre vines give a rich ripe mixture of wild fruit. The fruit transfers to a firm, rustic palate with notes of kirsch, leather and subtle oak. This Grande Réserve will transport you to the Languedoc hills when you taste it with lamb chops marinated in olive oil and thyme and grilled on a wood fire.

Wines €5.25-€10.80

Paul & Penelope Dudson
Château Haute-Fontaine,
Domaine de Java,
Prat de Cest, 11100 Bages
- Rooms: 4 twins/doubles, €55 per night. 3 gîtes for 2-6, €400-€1,200 per week.
- Meals: Restaurant 1km.
- Closed: January.
- +33 (0)4 68 41 03 73
- www.chateauhautefontaine.com

living cum dining room. There are two double bedrooms on the ground floor and a large attic room with four single beds. The décor and furnishings are unfussy: this is a family-friendly gîte. Two smaller apartments are in the stable block overlooking the courtyard. Les Lavandes is a perfect hideaway for two. Next door is the two-bedroom apartment Les Genets off the courtyard, with four bedrooms and available per night.

The grounds cover 300 hectares of wild garrigue and thirty of Corbières vineyards that are cultivated organically. Paul and Penny cultivate ten different grape varieties on the clay-limestone slopes in a climate tempered by sea breezes. They harvest the grapes by hand and machine. "We use both methods to get the best possible fruit," he says, "and delicate varieties or older vines are hand-picked." Traditional methods and modern, temperature-controlled techniques create excellent flavours.

Haute-Fontaine is a great place for discovering this 'New World' of French wines. There are, too, Mediterranean beaches and stunning scenery, fortified towns and hilltop villages and, best of all, you'll rarely find yourself in a crowd.

Château Ricardelle

AUDE

Long ago this land was drained for agriculture and growing vines but, even earlier, before the Gallo-Roman period, the Aude flowed into a large bay. In the middle of the delta a cluster of limestone peaks formed a great island – the Isle du Lac – whose southern Occitan name became La Clape. Today, a steep, narrow road zigzags its way to the top of the massif, from where you are rewarded with a fabulous panorama – of the Mediterranean sea, the hazy mountains of Spain, the cathedral city of Narbonne and, on the plain below, the Pellegrinis' château and winery.

More a cluster of charming buildings than a single grand château, Ricardelle is a tangle of stone façades, terracotta pantile roofs, sheltered courtyards and tree-shaded gardens. Asymmetrical, cubist, almost Braquesque, the 'chateau' has a history that is long but largely undocumented. Generations of masons have worked on this house and some projects have never been completed.

There's even an unfinished stone stairway – the stair was abandoned over a century ago!

Like so many winemakers in the Languedoc, the owners are new to the region. Francine arrived in 2001; Bruno continued working as a wine 'courtier' for a couple of years, then moved here. Francine explains their origins. "I'm from the Touraine, Bruno was born in the Italian Tyrol – we are both foreigners!" Between them the Pellegrinis speak French, English, Italian, German and Spanish – which is useful, because guests descend from many corners of the globe. And all fall in love with this very old house, set between the mountains and the sea.

The Pellegrinis have created three delightful gîtes in buildings that nudge the main house. Quarry tile floors and country kitchens express a simple rustic theme, while the thick limestone walls keep the rooms cool in the height of summer. Families can happily spread in Roussane, the

largest gîte, with two good double bedrooms, furnished with lovely Tyrolean pieces hand-painted by Bruno. In Grenache one of the bedrooms is on the ground floor, opening to a private courtyard. The smallest house, Carignan, is for two, with a pergola on a sun-baked patio. At the château are two more apartments: Syrah and Merlot.

Bruno and Francine attend to wedding parties as well as holidaymakers and eno-tourists. Newlyweds and up to 130 guests get a vast banqueting hall above the vat house in which to celebrate, except during harvest, when the room reverts to its main function as the loading area for the grapes that are tipped into the cavernous tanks below.

Around 40 hectares of AOC vines are cultivated on the limestone slopes of La Clape (mainly syrah, grenache and carignan) and eight further hectares classified as 'vins de pays'; these are planted with merlot, cabernet sauvignon and viognier. You get a fascinating mix of serious complex wines and modern, easy-drinkers, all of which can be tasted in the smart salon where grand chandeliers illuminate hundreds of bottles.

WINES

**Château Ricardelle, 'Le Blason'
Coteaux du Languedoc la Clape**
The vines, encouraged by record levels of sunshine, cooled by mountain breezes and drained by the gravely limestone soil, yield excellent fruit. This is a superb wine with a dense, aromatic black fruit aroma and a concentrated, structured palate. Reserve Bruno's top wine for a rich dish like Civet de Lièvre – wild hare marinated in red wine.

Wines €4.50–€25

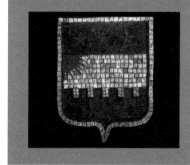

Francine & Bruno Pellegrini
Château Ricardelle,
Route de Gruissan,
11100 Narbonne
• Rooms: 5 gîtes for 2-6,
  €200-€800 per week.
• Meals: Restaurant 4km.
• Closed: Rarely.
• +33 (0)4 68 65 21 00
• www.chateau-ricardelle.com

Mas du Soleilla

AUDE

At first light the pickers are in the vines filling their crates with delicate bunches of red grapes. They work quickly and the small vineyard is finished by the time the sun peeps over the ridge. Carrying heavy crates in cold, grape-stained hands the team moves on to the next field to continue 'la vendange manuelle', the hand-picked harvest that is so important to the quality of La Clape wines.

Swiss couple Peter Wildbolz and Christa Derungs are the owners of Mas du Soleilla, a Provençal-syle country house surrounded by nineteen hectares of vines. Peter was in the wine trade and dreamed of having his own vineyard; Christa worked in high fashion and high-society catering, but was no less ambitious to become a winemaker. In 2002, in search of sunshine and vines, they bought this beautiful house, opened their B&B and started making wine. Christa explains what they set out to achieve. "Right from the start we wanted people to stay and to experience what we had discovered – a unique landscape, a wonderful climate, and great wine."

A nearby hill and the omnipresent sun gave the house its name; terraces, covered and open, overlook the vineyards and the Mediterranean Sea. Hard to believe that the house, constructed of local stone with adobe walls painted in warm earth colours, is only thirty years old. Each guest room has its own terrace leading to lawns where deckchairs sit beneath Aleppo pines. Indoors, walls and woodwork are painted in muted shades and terracotta floor tiles and fabrics in subtle colours produce an air of cool serenity.

Tantalising views of the Mediterranean will tempt you to explore. Whether in the saddle (mountain bikes are available) or on foot, the protected nature reserve of La Clape is a joy to discover. From the house, stone steps lead down into the organic vines; from there, a network of pebbly paths link the vineyards to the hills. You can climb the high

WINES

**Mas du Soleilla, 'Les Chailles'
Coteaux du Languedoc la Clape**
Harvested and sorted by hand, the grapes are of superb quality. This rich, fruity wine comes from the little vineyard of Les Chailles. Sweet blackcurrant and blackberry dominate the aroma and transfer to a smooth and sustaining finish. La Clape wines work well with spicy food and this goes very well with a mild curry.

Wines €6–€32

Christa Derungs & Peter Wildbolz
Mas du Soleilla,
Route de Narbonne Plage,
11100 Narbonne
- Rooms: 5 twins/doubles, €95–€135.
- Meals: Restaurant 1km.
- Closed: Never.
- +33 (0)4 68 45 24 80
- www.mas-du-soleilla.com

limestone peaks or descend to Narbonne beach. In the evening, amid the rich aroma of wild thyme, rosemary and lavender, a short stroll brings you to a chic modern restaurant.

Christa is an accomplished cook and she serves a generous and delicious breakfast on the terrace by the pool or in the ochre and sienna dining room. Try the local honey and the home-grown kumquats preserved in syrup; during harvest time there's freshly pressed grape juice.

Back in the winery the picked fruit arrives from the fields. "The grapes are harvested at the optimum moment of ripeness," explains Peter, over the din of the sorting-table's conveyer. "They are sorted twice – first bunch by bunch, then grape by grape." Thousands of grapes whizz by with each turn of the conveyer belt and those that don't pass muster are discarded. "We believe that the hands-on approach produces a fair wine," he says – modestly; his hand-made wines are superb. Taste them and you'll understand why Soleilla keeps winning regional trophies from Decanter and Wine Spectator.

Les Gîtes en Minervois

HÉRAULT

"We must indulge the mind and from time to time allow it the leisure which is its food and strength. We must go for walks, so that the mind can be strengthened and invigorated by a clear sky and plenty of fresh air. At times it will acquire fresh energy from a change of scene, or from socialising and drinking freely."

So wrote Seneca the Younger, Roman statesman and stoic, two millennia ago. Inspired by this philosophy of travel and social fulfilment, a couple of Burgundian winemakers set off on a quest to find a new vineyard.

Anne Gros and Jean-Paul Tollot live with their three children in Burgundy's Côte d'Or. They both inherited family vineyards and produce fabulous wines in both the Côte de Nuits and the Côte de Beaune. In 2008, pooling the know-how of their dynasties, they found their new domaine, not in Burgundy, but in the wild, rugged landscape under

the "clear sky" of the Minervois. Their new venture is near Aigues Vives, on the edge of the Haut Languedoc regional park.

A dozen hectares of Minervois vines surround a purpose-built eco winery made from timber and insulating brick. The building, like the Ark atop Mount Ararat, sits at the head of the vineyard slopes, its wooden walls, convex roof sections and balustraded 'deck' creating a nautical feel. Wasn't it Noah who planted the first vine?

The vat room and barrel cellar are down below; aloft are a spacious apartment and two small studios. The views to the mountains in the heat-hazy distance are wondrous. Anne and Jean-Paul intended just to create lodgings for their seasonal workers but the rooms would have been unused for most of the year so they opened them to tourists too."

There's a touch of urban chic about the gîtes. The apartment Grand Carignan has a modern

WINES

Domaine Anne Gros et Jean-Paul Tollot, Minervois
This is a new winery and we tasted the wines before the final blending and bottling but the old-vine carignan, syrah and grenache cuvées offered a promising preview of the finished blend. To the normally robust and fruity reds, Anne and Jean-Paul are adding a touch of Burgundy finesse. Should be perfect with a rich beef dish such as boeuf en daube.

open-plan kitchen, two large bedrooms, a sofabed for children and a broad terrace. Spacious and light, the neutral colour scheme creates a zen-like calm; a dash of burgundy adds a vibrancy. Cleverly compact, the studios, each sleeping four, are great value, and share a terrace.

Find a moment to visit Jean-Paul's brand-new winery where the wines wait patiently in shiny steel vats. "Our first vintage, from the harvest of 2008, has still not been released," he explains, sampling a taste of the nascent Minervois red from the barrel. "Everything here is new, except the vines. We will restructure the vineyards and replant a few but hold on to the ninety-year-old carignan vines." He's a big fan of the carignan grape which, after years of decline, is finding favour once more; the fruit of the ancient vines is exceptional.

The Languedoc is a vast, diverse region. Sheer gorges and the story of the Cathars' macabre defeat will tempt you to explore the nearby village of Minerve, there's market day at Aigues Vives for the lushest local produce, mountain wilderness to the north, and the Med to the south.

Anne Gros & Jean Paul Tollot
Les Gîtes en Minervois,
Rue du Couchant, Cazellles,
34210 Aigues Vives
- Rooms: 3 gîtes for 2-6, €300-€600 per week.
- Meals: Restaurant 3km.
- Closed: Rarely.
- +33 (0)3 80 61 07 95
- www.anne-gros.com

Les Amants de la Vigneronne

HÉRAULT

Hailing from the inclement Brabant, Régine and Christian Godefroid were drawn to the south by the climate. "It rains rather a lot in Belgium so we came in search of the sun." They ended up with more than sunshine: a whole new life in a hilly land 'twixt mountains and sea', plus vineyard.

La Vigneronne is a grand 19th-century house with blue shutters on the edge of the wine village of Faugères. When the couple arrived it was in a parlous state but Christian and Régine beavered away, and so successfully that by the end of the first year they had restored the main house and created five B&B rooms. Next, five hectares of vineyards needed attention. "We opened the winery in 2003 and our first vintage was in 2004," says Régine.

From the courtyard you enter a snug salon and a dining room built into the old winery vaults. A crackling fire in the grate of a large cheminée illuminates old bottles and country bric-a-brac, while shadows dance on rustic walls. In contemporary bedrooms are new terracotta-tiled floors, original oak-beamed ceilings and the occasional wall of exposed stone, meticulously restored. Voile-hung four-poster beds add softness, a canopy ring was crafted from an old wine barrel, and restored oak doors open to bathrooms, one with a spa bath.

Régine serves dinner by the fire on cool evenings but most of the year they eat outside. Ask, and she'll give you a recipe: "Good food does not need to be complicated." The entrée she cooked for us is an excellent example: Pélardon goat's cheese sprinkled with pepper and thyme, a touch of garlic and a drizzle of honey, served on salad leaves with a light vinaigrette. Breakfast is a tasty array of fresh bread and homemade conserves (fig, quince, cherry, lemon) – and, as befits a proper Belgian household, chocolate and cheese.

Christian has named his small winery Les Amants (The Lovers). His wines, too, have sensual names. "Yes, I choose

WINES

**Les Amants de la Vigneronne,
'De Chair et de Sang' Faugères**
A leg of lamb, slowly oven-roasted with garlic, thyme and rosemary begs for a full, juicy southern red. Christian's wine is just the ticket: a blend of deeply coloured mourvèdre and firm, concentrated grenache make a full bodied wine bursting with lively fruit. You'll find aromas of almond and vanilla, white pepper and dark chocolate.

Wines €6–€22.50

Régine & Christian Godefroid
Les Amants de la Vigneronne,
La Vigneronne, 18 route de Pézenas,
34600 Faugères
• Rooms: 5 twins/doubles, €74–€106.
• Meals: Dinner, with wine €32.
• Closed: 15 November–15 February.
• +33 (0)4 67 95 78 49
• www.lavigneronne.com

unusual names for my wines," he admits, as he pours a generous glass of De Chair et De Sang (Flesh and Blood). "This is a full-bodied wine that gets its plenitude ('la chair') from the grenache grape and its cardinal colour ('le sang') from the mourvèdre." As for the intensely dark Rouge aux Lèvres (Blood on the Lips), its inspiration was an old vampire film. The name of Christian's juiciest white wine, Soif de Toi (Thirst for You), is taken from a psalm. Visit the boutique and wine bar in the vaults where they stock wines from each of Faugères' producers.

La Vigneronne's wines are grown organically and the harvest is done by hand. Each autumn, friends work from first light to bring in the crop and Régine keeps them going with supplies of coffee. After a hard day's harvesting (or exploring) it's comforting to know you can come back here. Take a dip in La Vigneronne's pool or find a seat in the shady courtyard for a moment's contemplation. Or visit Faugères' Les Trois Tours, an amazing three-towered windmill (still functioning) on a windswept hill with stupendous views.

Domaine de Saint Ferréol

HÉRAULT

Jorje and Ania are seasoned travellers. Born in England, both to Polish families, they lived and worked overseas for many years before settling in the Hérault valley. Jorje was destined to work in the vines: a PhD in chemistry launched a career in food technology and his professional wine travels took him to Bordeaux, Burgundy, Slovenia, Hungary, Georgia and Bulgaria. In 1998 they bought a neglected priory near Pézenas. Now they seldom travel; Saint Ferréol is, for them, the home that "our feet may leave, but not our hearts".

"We came here to create the sort of place we most appreciated during our travels," says Ania, "a beautiful and comfortable place run by friendly hosts to add a personal touch." What they have achieved is much more. Enveloped by fourteen hectares of park and woodland, the property has more than just vines. Sunny lawns and shady trees surround a large pool where wheeling swifts skim

the surface at sunset. Nesting eagle owls, a trout stream and a wildlife pond in the woods are natural lures for young nature-loving children; there's a play area too, with a giant trampoline and ball games. The enclosed courtyard of the 12th-century priory is alive with tropical flora: plantain and persimmon thrive, bougainvillea romps.

Within the quadrangle's ancient walls are six large villas each with independent access and a private terrace or garden. The one-, two- and three-bedroom villas are bright; in each, the living room opens onto the terrace for outdoor dining. "Each year brings over 300 days of sunshine and we eat outside," says Jorje. Antique and country furniture, traditional Catalan fireplaces and oak-and-terracotta floors complement the priory's exposed stone walls and wooden beams.

For a glimpse into the long and fascinating history of the house you need only to descend into

the cellars. An ancient well, in the depths of the cool vat house, is the last vestige of a Roman villa that once stood here. The foundations date back to the ninth century and the medieval priory, dedicated to the Bishop of Uzès, was built around 1140. Saint Ferréol's more recent winemaking history looms large in the winery: a row of twelve foot high oak vats – 'foudres' – that once fermented hundreds of hectolitres of wine. Today, Jorje uses modern vats to make his wines, then ages them in small oak barrels. The old foudres, too big to move, stay here and create a fitting backdrop for Jorje's wine tastings.

Every morning the baker arrives (listen for her klaxon). For other groceries, head for Pézenas, five kilometres away. Molière lived and worked here and the medieval town has a rich history. Throughout the summer Pézenas celebrates its festival of arts and music and its Saturday market is a brilliant place to buy fresh local produce (as well as artisan crafts and brocante). You can horse ride on the golden Mediterranean beaches, canoe down the canyons of the Herault gorge, bird watch in the marshes of the Camargue.

WINES

**Domaine de Saint Ferréol,
Vin de Pays d'Oc**
Viognier is such a fruity and floral varietal: the bouquet of citrus and apricot, white flowers and honey capture the grapes' essence and precede a rich but fresh mouthful of zesty flavours. A tad of residual sweetness makes this a perfect aperitif wine; it is also a good accompaniment to local dishes such as aiguillettes of duck cooked in honey, orange and cumin.
Wines from €9.85

Jorje & Ania Maslakiewicz
Domaine de Saint Ferréol,
34320 Nizas
- Rooms: 6 gîtes for 2-6, €490–€1,850 per week.
- Meals: Restaurant 3km.
- Closed: Rarely.
- +33 (0)4 67 25 28 32
- www.stferreol.com

Domaine Saint Hilaire
HÉRAULT

An ex-barrister (Queen's Counsel) and a film agent for Monty Python: these are the unlikely owners of the Domaine Saint Hilaire. Between the oyster-pooled shores of Lake Thau and the lively town of Pézenas is an 18th-century bastide surrounded by 200 acres of vines – a supremely elegant home and a remarkable winery.

Jonathan and Anne James were living in the hills of the Montagne Noire before their desire to become vignerons brought them to Saint Hilaire. They bought winery, house and vineyards in 2002 and released their first vintage soon after. The judges of the revered French wine guide Hachette were so taken by the wine that they awarded it top marks; astonishment turned to delight when further plaudits came their way. "But pride in our successes came before the proverbial fall," says Anne candidly. "The roof above the vats collapsed during a heavy storm and

we produced the 2004 vintage in a winery that was open to the skies."

The property was beautifully restored, the vineyards were restructured and the winery got a new roof. Visitors, charmed by the house, suggested this would make a perfect spot for a B&B and so, in 2007, they opened up four ultra-elegant guest rooms, each named after one of the winds of the Hérault: Levant, Autun, Terral and, of course, Mistral. Old Provençal floor tiles, painted mouldings and exposed oak timbers sing the history; chaises longues, a theatrical four-poster and big wet rooms add great comfort. The library, where films are sometimes screened (including the much-loved Pythons) reverts to a quiet place for reading. Five o'clock tea is served in the living room; at seven, pre-dinner apéritifs. Doors from here and from the adjoining dining room open to a sunny terrace and the sound of the 'infinity' pool. Wonderful.

WINES

Domaine Saint Hilaire, 'Advocate' Vin de Pays d'Oc

A blend of cabernet sauvignon and merlot grapes make a square-shouldered Bordeaux-style red with a spicy southern twist. The Spanish influences that brought bull-running and flamenco to the Languedoc also brought paella; the classic Catalan dish goes very well with the Advocate's mix of black fruits and smoky, torrefied aromas. Try the rosé with poached figs and raspberries.
Wines €4.50–€12

Anne & Jonathan James
Domaine Saint Hilaire,
34530 Montagnac

- Rooms: 4 doubles, €125–€190.
- Meals: Dinner with wine, €40.
- Closed: Rarely.
- +33 (0)4 67 24 00 08
- www.domainesaint-hilaire.com

An amiable and gracious host, Anne does everything to make you feel looked after. There are bowls of fresh fruit in the bedrooms, morning tea and coffee are brought to your room, and the lavish buffet breakfast lingers until eleven o'clock. On Monday evenings, when French restaurants often close, you can sample Anne's regional cooking, which includes picked-that-day vegetables from the potager. You can eat in the dining room by a crackling fire, or in the jasmine-scented gardens beneath a starry Languedoc sky.

A half-hour drive brings you to the pretty harbour of Mèze, and then to the fishing port of Sète. Running through the town is the 17th-century Canal du Midi, an engineering marvel, now a world heritage site – a conduit for pleasure boats between the Atlantic and the Mediterranean.

Wine is Jonathan's passion. "We wanted to produce a world-class vin de pays, and we have been helped by talented people." His top wines, Advocate and Silk, are a testament to his success. The whites are clean and fresh, the reds, whose grapes ripen over a hundred sun-soaked days, ooze rich, ripe fruit.

RHÔNE VALLEY & PROVENCE

RHÔNE VALLEY & PROVENCE

Provence! The name evokes images of sunshine and olive groves, fields of lavender and vineyards. Cézanne and Van Gogh captured its beauty in the 19th century; novels like 'Jean de Florette' and 'A Year in Provence' popularised it in the 20th. From the mountains to the sea, many rivers shape a landscape of gorges and peaceful valleys. One river, above all, dominates: the Rhône.

The Celts called it the Great River. Born in the glacial ice of the Swiss Alps, it follows an 800km journey ending in a broad delta on the shores of the Mediterranean. On its way south it carves the steeply terraced slopes of the Côte Rôtie and the hills of Tain-l'Heritage. At Montélimar, the 'gates of Provence', vine growing gives way to the production of nougat (one of the thirteen desserts of the traditional Provençal Christmas) but the vines return further south and cover the 'coteaux' of the Ardèche and Tricastin.

The river flows past the Côtes-du-Rhône villages of Chateauneuf-du-Pape, Gigondas and Vacqueyras and beneath the broken arches of the Pont d'Avignon. At Arles, it splits and the Petit Rhône, separated from its big brother, forms the boundary between the Costières de Nîmes vineyards and the marshland of the Camargue. East of Avignon, the snow-capped summit of Mont Ventoux surveys its vines and, next to them, those of the beautiful Luberon hills. This is the real Provence of rugged peaks and the wild garrigue. Vines are grown from Aix-en-Provence, in the Bouches du Rhône, to the resort town of Saint Raphaël on the Côte d'Azur. At Nice there is a tiny hilltop appellation called Bellet, the most south-easterly of all France's vineyards.

Climate and landscape shape the region's food: fish and seafood from the shores of the Mediterranean and lamb, game and goat's milk cheese from the upland hills. Olives (and the finest olive oil), sun-ripened vegetables and citrus fruits provide the basic ingredients for tapenade, ratatouille and the beef stew, daube Provençal. Salted anchovies give flavour and seasoning to dishes like salade niçoise and pissaladière – ideal hot weather snacks made even more delicious with a glass of chilled rosé wine.

Many styles of wine are available to match the region's varied cuisine. Some of France's finest and most long-lived red wines come from the vineyards near Vienne, Valence and Avignon. You'll discover sparkling crémants near the town of Die, exemplary sweet whites at Condrieu and fortified wines at Beaumes-de-Venise. Fine wines of all colours can be found in the Côtes-du-Ventoux and the Côtes-du-Luberon, and the appellations of the Côtes-de-Provence, long associated with pale summertime rosés, produce some excellent dry whites and full-bodied reds, too.

In our Provençal properties you can spend a week in a fabulous gîte or apartment or tour the region while based in B&Bs. At grand medieval châteaux and on small, family farms, you can enjoy classical music events, cookery classes and wine courses and discover the first organic village in France. The region's other delights include Avignon, the city of the Popes and Anti-Popes; the Roman arenas of Arles and Orange; the multi-ethnic city of Marseilles and the wild beauty of the Camargue.

Château de la Tuilerie

GARD

Caesar's legions, returning from the Egyptian wars, were given lands here, on the fertile plain of Nîmes. Beautifully preserved, the amphitheatre and aqueduct recall the city's majestic history and in the fields all around grows another Roman legacy: the grapevine.

On a gentle rise of north-facing vineyards between the city and the sea is one of the southern Rhône's most celebrated wine properties. Chateau de la Tuilerie is the family estate of Chantal Comte, a progressive and charismatic winemaker with a passion for art and culture. Her wine labels are adorned with fine art motifs, open-air recitals fill the summer evening air with music, and original works deck the walls of the Bastide – a stylish and opulent holiday house in the heart of the vineyards.

La Bastide de Fabrègues is a prestigious 18th-century building in a beautiful walled garden where oleanders and English roses flourish. In coral pink, with a balconied first floor above a wrought-iron arcade, the house has a serene, colonial charm. Behind the stone walls, a cool, bright interior includes a large living room full of deep sofas, and a peaceful well-stocked library. For informal dining you have a butler's pantry kitchen; for grand dinners, a large dining room with an oak refectory table. Upstairs are three big double bedrooms furnished with fine antiques and decorated with paintings and engravings. The king-size beds are dressed with hand-embroidered cotton percale and each room opens onto a sunny balcony looking down onto the Orangery and the lily pond. Within the grounds you can bathe in a pristine circular pool or snooze in a hammock strung between century-old trees.

A twenty-minute walk from the Bastide takes you through the vineyards and past the château to the wine-tasting cellar. Chantal knows her wines and her rums; she bottles fine aged rum from the island of Marie-Galante in

Guadeloupe. Chantal is an anglophile with family living in London and speaks fluent English; teatime is one of her favourite things. "For nearly thirty years I've been the guardian of my wines and rums, and I like to describe them provocatively and poetically".

The land here is ideal for vine cultivation: the soil is poor, acidic and free-draining and, in this hot climate, the vines benefit from their northerly orientation. "Nature provides the potential, but hard work, knowledge and time are needed to make truly great wine," says Chantal. "You also need to add love, care, attention – and need to take pleasure in the process." Chantal's wines and rums are certainly a great pleasure to taste.

A week's stay in the pampered surroundings of La Bastide will give you ample opportunity to enjoy the estate's wines but there's more to the region than viticulture. The Camargue countryside lends itself to cycling – so discover the wild horses and the black bulls, and the mysterious dry stone 'capitelles' that have provided shelter for centuries.

WINES

Château de la Tuilerie, 'Grenache Blanc/Viognier' Costières de Nimes
Northerly Mistral winds and sea breezes from the coastal plain cool the vines and create the fresh, lively character of this grenache/viognier blend. Aromas of white blossom, peach and peardrops leap out of the glass. Refreshing as an aperitif, serve it cool as a lunchtime accompaniment to a terrine of Provençal vegetables with a light basil and yogurt dressing.
Wines €7–€30

Chantal Comte
Château de la Tuilerie – La Bastide de Fabrègues, 571 chemin de la Tuilerie, 30900 Nimes
- Rooms: 1 gîte for 6, €2,000–€3,000 per week.
- Meals: Restaurant 3km.
- Closed: Never.
- +33 (0)4 66 70 07 52
- www.labastidedefabregues.com

Domaine de Bournet

ARDÈCHE

Château de Bournet's vineyards lie between the banks of the river Chassezac and the village of Grospierres. A few kilometres downstream, the river joins the Ardèche and forms a mighty torrent that cuts its way through canyons and under the natural limestone archway of the Pont d'Arc. The area is popular with tourists for its dramatic landscapes and Mediterranean climate; the wines of the Coteaux de l'Ardèche are less well known.

In 1755 Olivier de Bournet's ancestors were granted the right to grow vines here. He and his father Xavier make the wines in the cellars of the 15th-century bastide Mas-Neuf. "Here this is not considered such an old building," Olivier explains, "so it's still known as the new farm!" Less than a kilometre away is an even older property – La Ferme de Bournet – where Olivier's aunt and uncle run the hotel and restaurant.

Like a small hamlet, La Ferme is a rural citadel in stone. The ancient buildings form two courtyards which lead to the rooms, apartments and gîtes. Choose between the stone-vaulted bedchambers in the old wine cellars, or the light, colourful upstairs bedrooms. Such variety, such character! The décor is embellished with elegant curtains and boutis bedspreads; there's a large suite with room for six, too.

There are also one- and two-bedroom apartments and cottages: Voidon has a beautiful checkerboard floor, exposed beams and an authentic country kitchen; Tanargue, a cottage for four, a super spiral staircase to a mezzanine. In all: seven gites and eight hotel rooms and a real sense of privacy and independence. You can stroll round a small lake in the wooded park, relax by the pool, or explore the hundreds of hectares.

Madame de Bournet is the chef de cuisine in the great vaulted restaurant, her husband, Edouard, serves the wine, and other family

Photos: Adrien Louche

members wait on. Traditional, regional dishes go perfectly with the estate's Vins de Pays reds and whites; try a fillet of poached trout with a saffron sauce and a glass of aromatic viognier, or a seven-hour cooked gigot of lamb with a soft and fruity merlot.

The winery is a ten-minute walk; stepping out of the scorching sun and into the cool vaulted wine cellar is pure delight! Xavier and Olivier farm twenty-three hectares of organic vines planted with a mix of cabernet, merlot and syrah for the reds, and viognier and chardonnay for the whites. Carthagène, a rare local aperitif, is made here too. "Some bottles have lasted over a hundred years," Olivier reveals. Aromas of apricot, pineapple, fig and raisins make it a delicious aperitif or dessert wine.

Explore the river gorges by kayak, ride in the hills or visit the cathedral-like caverns of Orgnac. The sense of prehistory is palpable: Stone Age cave dwellings, menhirs and dolmens abound. At the Grotte de Chauvet, a child's footprints, preserved for over 25,000 years, are even more poignant than the beautiful cave paintings left by her forebears.

WINES

Domaine de Bournet, 'Cuvée Chris'
Vin de Pays des Coteaux de l'Ardèche
A mix of cabernet sauvignon and merlot vines, planted nearly 30 years ago give, respectively, the spice and the fruit to this oak-aged red. Aromas of capsicum, cherry and spices plus hints of vanilla and toast combine beautifully. Serve it, not too warm, with a hot, spicy dish. Wonderful with that princely French Maghreb feast, Couscous Royal.
Wines €6.50–€15

Olivier de Bournet
Domaine de Bournet,
07120 Grospierres
- Rooms: 8: 3 doubles, 3 triples,
  1 quadruple, 1 suite for 6, €60–€140.
  7 gîtes for 3-6, €350–€790 per week.
- Meals: Breakfast €8. Dinner €26–€36.
- Closed: January-February.
- +33 (0)4 75 39 68 20
- www.domaine-de-bournet.com

Domaine Saint Luc

DRÔME

In the heart of the Drôme Provençale, at the northern end of the Côtes du Rhône, the slopes of the Coteaux du Tricastin form a patchwork of lavender fields, truffle-scented woodland and vines. After years of working in other people's cellars and vineyards, two couples – the Cooks and the Hémards – arrived to look after these vines.

"It was one of those moments of madness," says Stéphane Hémard, "where we allowed our passions to lead us and ended up with this beautiful 18th-century 'mas' and twenty-eight hectares of vineyards." Stéphane and his wife Pascale live in nearby Avignon, but Rémi and Estelle Cook settled here in 2006: he looks after the winery and she the guests. The farmhouse, whose lintel is engraved with the year 1769, has four bed and breakfast rooms. Conservation rather than renovation has resulted in an authentic interior: note the original parfeuille terracotta tiles set in ceilings, oak posts and beams. Small windows in the north-facing walls protect the bedrooms from summer heat and winter Mistral; simple, high quality furnishings and antiques create a cosy, elegant mood. The rustic theme stops short of the bathrooms: these are modern and large.

The gîtes are a few paces from the main house. Bacchus, the larger of the two, has room for an extra single bed; Dionysus has a pergola-shaded terrace. There's a super pool, an area for friendly communal meals, a children's play space and acres of wooded garrigue. Not far away are the mighty castles of Suze and Grignan; these, and numerous Romanesque chapels, can be explored via a circuit of cycle paths.

Rémi's surname reveals his Anglo-Saxon ancestry: he comes from a long line of Protestant ministers, originally from England, who settled in this stronghold of French Protestantism. La Beaume de Transit is so-called because, in

WINES

Domaine Saint Luc, 'L'Escale Sérine'
Côtes du Rhône Villages
Sérine is the northern Rhône name for the syrah grape that dominates this concentrated and complex wine. A wild, ripe, almost jammy fruit carries with it subtle aromas of flowers and a hint of liquorice. The supple palate and slight bitterness should pair nicely with a grilled entrecôte steak smothered in black olive butter and roasted shallots.

Wines €5.50–€14

DOMAINE
SAINT LUC
2005
L'ESCALE SÉRIN
CÔTES DU RHÔNE VILLAGES

Estelle & Remi Cook,
Pascale & Stéphane Hémard
Domaine Saint Luc,
26790 La Baume-de-Transit
● Rooms: 4 twins/doubles, €65–€98.
  2 gîtes for 2–5, €375–€597 per week.
● Meals: Restaurant 3km.
● Closed: Never.
● +33 (0)4 75 98 11 51
● dom-saint-luc.com

the 16th-century, it was a frontier town between the Drôme in the Protestant north and Provence in the Catholic south. Rémi spent his early childhood in South Africa and both he and Estelle speak English. After a spell working in the Dominican Republic, the couple came back to France. "Saint Luc enables us to share our enthusiasm for wine with our visitors. We offer tours, winemaking courses and tasting events," says Estelle.

The vineyards cover twenty-eight hectares in the Coteaux de Tricastin and Côtes du Rhône Villages appellations. Rémi explains how each area, so close in geography, produces such distinctive wines. "Tricastin grapes grown in sandy, soft clay soils give an elegance and freshness, while the heavy red clays in our Rhône vineyards retain the day's heat and produce a rich and spicy wine." Inspired by the northern Rhône tradition of adding white viognier to red wine, Rémi adds a little of this aromatic grape to his Tricastin 'Excellence'. Few people guess this mystery ingredient; he'll be impressed if you detect it.

Le Clos du Caveau

VAUCLUSE

At daybreak, all is silent in the broad valley. Chickens shake the cool night from their feathers and wait for the shadows cast by the high crags to recede and reveal the wakening vines. In the middle of the vineyards is a rambling 18th-century farm, built from the same pale stone that forms the peaks of the Dentelles de Montmirail above. This idyllic Provençal house is home to a remarkable family of winemakers.

Gérard Bungener discovered Le Clos de Caveau in 1976 and embarked on an adventure that was to change his and his family's lives. He began by restoring the old house and the winery; everyone joined in and many friends made the journey up the narrow lane from Vacqueyras to help. The renovations were particularly onerous for Gérard who suffered from a severe form of arthritis. Having tried many treatments, he finally consulted a naturopath who cured him with a strict, natural

diet. This almost miraculous recovery inspired Gérard to cultivate his vines organically, but covertly: at that time 'organic' was considered inferior in wine circles.

After Gérard retired in 2005, his son and his Scottish wife took over the Domaine. "We were living in London, Henri had just got his PhD and the children were settled in school – but this place won us over," says Janet. Next to the main house is a charming small cottage for two, from whose small leafy terrace you enter a Provençal kitchen. White stucco and lime-washed oak maximise the pale light that penetrates the shuttered windows; up an ancient oak and brick staircase is the small bathroom. On the terrace (cool and shady during the day, warmed by the evening sun) are a small table and chairs, and guests are welcome to bathe in the family's pool next door. The other two gîtes are a few minutes walk from the village, at the .

WINES

Domaine Le Clos de Caveau, Vacqueyras
Like a prize-fighter in a silk suit, Henri's powerful wines also have elegance and charm. Approachable yet structured, the damson fruit aromas, the whiff of herbes de Provence and the palate of black fruits and spicy liquorice call for a hearty, aromatic dish. Serve it with a meaty Daube Provençal, redolent of black olives, orange and thyme.

Wines €5–€25

LE CLOS DE CAVEAU VACQUEYRAS
CRU DES CÔTES DU RHÔNE
CARMIN BRILLANT 2006

Janet Bungener
Le Clos du Caveau,
Chemin de Caveau, 84190 Vacqueyras
- Rooms: 3 gîtes for 2-10,
  €400–€1,600 per week.
- Meals: Restaurant 4km.
- Closed: Never.
- +33 (0)4 90 65 85 33
- www.vacation-rentals-provence.com

southern end of the vines and surrounded by them. They share a decked terrace and a large pool. Modern houses, they have been constructed from traditional materials, then very simply, very beautifully, furnished. They have big living rooms, log-burning inglenooks and colourful minimalist kitchens.

"A vineyard is part of the natural world," Henri says, "and we encourage the interaction with nature – the wild plants and animals all contribute something to the health and quality of the vines, even if some wildlife can be a nuisance."

Thyme and rosemary flourish at the margins of the stony vineyard and herbal and mineral characteristics have been noted by some of the wine world's top commentators. Robert Parker (the American critic) found "garrigue and spice" in the bouquet; Oz Clarke described the taste of "sun-drenched grape juice...run over a bed of stones". Henri's daughter Rose insists she can detect the aroma of herbes de Provence in the glass; her sweet-toothed little brother Lewis suggests planting strawberries between the vines...

Fine, organic wines, genuine, friendly people and charming gîtes. An irresistible combination

Le Paradou

VAUCLUSE

In the lee of Mont Ventoux is a fabulous château winery. Château Pesquié's history connects the ancient world via Renaissance fiefdoms to the author Daudet and to three generations of the Bastide-Chaudière family. Edith Chaudière's parents bought the estate in the 1970s from an heir to the 19th-century writer's estate. A pioneering couple, they restructured the vineyards and began the estate's renewal.

Edith and her husband Paul left medical careers to take over the estate in the mid-1980s, built an amazing subterranean vat house and barrel cellar and began producing Côtes de Ventoux wines under their own label.

'Pesquié' is old Provençal and refers to the natural springs discovered here by the first Roman settlers, and wine artefacts dating from the period prove the importance of the vine in the area 2,000 years ago. Fifteen fountains spout and splash in the immaculate grounds of the house, a symmetrical bastide amid cedars of Lebanon and 200-year-old plane trees. The winery and cellars are a joy to visit and visitors can stay in a delightful restored water mill a couple of minutes' drive from the château.

Le Paradou is an 18th-century farm and mill surrounded by vines, olive trees and holm oaks. The house combines opulence with comfort and a wonderful feeling of space: two large double rooms on the ground floor, each with direct access to a private terrace, and two more below. Hand-painted antique furniture, walls in the warm colours of the Midi and cool tiled floors set the Mediterranean mood. A few acres of woodland surrounding the mill make an exciting playground for young explorers (timid wild boar have been spotted) and, for bathers, there's a large sunny pool on a secluded rise above the house.

Not far from Le Paradou are the estate's vineyards. A unique terroir produce a distinctive wine, praised by pundits like Jancis Robinson; Robert Parker described Pesquié as "the finest

estate in the Côtes de Ventoux". Edith explains how the vineyards and the Ventoux valley influence their wines. "The vines grow here at the crossroads between two weather systems – Alpine and Mediterranean – so they enjoy warm days and cool nights, refreshed by colder air descending from the snow-topped mountain. This microclimate, and the clay-limestone gravelly soils, are what gives our wines such personality."

Apart from the many wine-based activities, the winery hosts a busy summer season of painting and sculpture exhibitions and for two days the château grounds are transformed into a market of local crafts and produce. Walkers can follow a marked hike from the château through the vineyards; if you're feeling more adventurous you can climb Mont Ventoux and marvel at how the riders of the Tour de France manage to ascend its 2,000-metre summit. The Rhône villages of Chateauneuf-du-Pape, Vacqueyras and Gigondas are all within a short and scenic drive, as are Avignon and the coast. To the west: the wild Camargue and Roman Nîmes, birthplace of Alphonse Daudet who, wisely, made Pesquié his summer retreat.

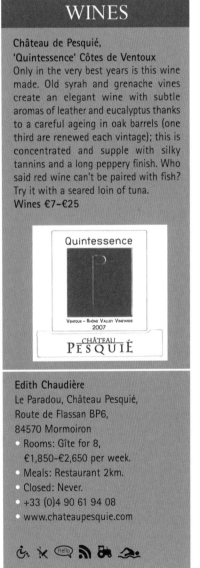

WINES

**Château de Pesquié,
'Quintessence' Côtes de Ventoux**
Only in the very best years is this wine made. Old syrah and grenache vines create an elegant wine with subtle aromas of leather and eucalyptus thanks to a careful ageing in oak barrels (one third are renewed each vintage); this is concentrated and supple with silky tannins and a long peppery finish. Who said red wine can't be paired with fish? Try it with a seared loin of tuna.
Wines €7–€25

Quintessence
VENTOUX – RHÔNE VALLEY VINEYARDS
2007
CHÂTEAU
PESQUIÉ

Edith Chaudière
Le Paradou, Château Pesquié,
Route de Flassan BP6,
84570 Mormoiron
• Rooms: Gîte for 8,
  €1,850–€2,650 per week.
• Meals: Restaurant 2km.
• Closed: Never.
• +33 (0)4 90 61 94 08
• www.chateaupesquie.com

Château Saint Estève de Néri

VAUCLUSE

Near the village of Ansouis, on the broad plains between the Luberon mountains and the river Durance, is small wine estate called Saint Estève de Néri. Allan and Alex Wilson discovered this beautiful Provençal farmhouse and winery in 2001 and fell in love with it – who wouldn't? In the embrace of vines and lavender in the heart of the impressive Luberon countryside, this estate is a rural idyll.

Allan and Alex are a friendly couple: he's Scottish and she is from Canada. They bought a holiday house here twenty years ago and, in 2001, came to spend "a year in Provence" (Peter Mayle's village, Ménerbes, is half an hour away). They gave up their City careers and moved with their two young children and their dog. As testimony to all their hard work, all who stay succumb to the charm of this joyously rambling property, its gardens and its beguiling little cottage.

Tucked between the winery and the main house, the red-shuttered cottage is a ground-floor space with enough room for two couples. From a sheltered patio in the gardens with views of the Luberon mountains you step into a small salon with comfy chairs and seagrass mats on an age-worn quarry tile floor. Original paintings by talented friends hang on walls painted in muted shades; ancient oak beams frame an open doorway into a cosy rustic kitchen with a small dining table. A smart, contemporary shower room is shared by the two double bedrooms.

The Wilsons also own a holiday home thirty minutes away in Goult where twelve people can enjoy unbridled pampering in a Provençal bastide. This farmhouse is also the setting for Alex's cookery courses; Allan organises wine tuition and his speciality is matching foods to wines.

Château Saint Estève de Néri, 'Grande Réserve' Côtes de Luberon
Another medal-winning red – this won silver in the Decanter world wine awards. Thirty-year-old vines, careful selection and a year in barriques results in a delicious bouquet of rich blackcurrant fruit and oak. The concentrated, elegant palate ends on a fresh, appley finish and goes superbly well with a rolled roast lamb stuffed with fresh herbes de Provence gathered from the garden.
Wines €7–€12

Warmed by the Mediterranean, the vineyards here are protected from the Mistral and cooled by the Luberon mountains to the north. A mixture of sandy light soil and heavier clay sit above cretaceous limestone and the climate and the terroir are ideal for growing organic vines. However, as Allan recalls, "our first harvest in 2002 was disastrous. Mother nature seemed to be against us and we had torrential rain during the harvest season." The following year brought an almost unbearable heatwave. But this time the wine was good, so good that it won a gold medal at the Concours Général in Paris.

Allan plans to achieve full organic status in 2010. "When we came there were no birds here at all. After a couple of years of organic farming they flocked back. Organic methods have brought more than great-tasting wines, then, so pick up the binoculars from your gîte and set out on a wildlife watch across the twenty hectares. You can play tennis here, too, or cycle to the magical, early medieval castle at Ansouis. A gentle evening swim in the secluded, heated pool back in Saint Estève's herb-scented gardens is the perfect prelude to an evening aperitif.

Allan & Alex Wilson
Château Saint Estève de Néri,
84240 Ansouis
- Rooms: Gîte for 4, €500–€1,000. Gîte for 12, €3,000–€6,250 (30-min drive). Prices per week.
- Meals: Restaurant 2km.
- Closed: Rarely.
- +33 (0)4 90 09 90 16
- www.stestevedeneri.com

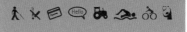

Château de Clapier

VAUCLUSE

Photo: Jacques Hertay

The landscape is familiar to those who love Provence, and to readers of Jean Giono, author of 'The Man Who Planted Trees' and other stories. There are hilltop villages and olive groves, lavender plantations and cherry orchards, and, on every stony slope, the vines.

Château de Clapier sits on the right bank of the river Durance and on the old post road from Manosque to Aix-en-Provence, and makes wonderful Côtes de Luberon wines. Its smart guesthouse Le Relais – once a very grand 18th-century post-house and a relais de poste – has an almost monastic feel with its pale stone walls and vaulted stone ceilings. In the eleven apartments, varying in size from one to four bedrooms each, the décor is classically French provençal: rustic yet smart. Each has its own high-spec kitchen, with a terrace or private garden, and bathrooms are colourful and contemporary with large walk-in showers.

The chambres d'hôtes rooms are full of colour and character. Downstairs are some impressive reception rooms: the vaulted salon and reading room, the dining room, and a little chapel (the priest comes once a week). And there's a large kitchen where guests can enjoy one of the regular cookery courses hosted by Clapier's associate chef, Caroline Miquel.

Thomas Montagne's ancestor bought the estate in 1880. Several generations have made wine here and Thomas has been the head of the domaine since 1995. He's a friendly, independent vigneron who believes that wine-making starts in the vineyard: "bad grapes never made good wine," says he. His family were technical innovators from the start (they installed an early steam-powered de-stemming machine) and he continues to use the best modern techniques with the "wisdom of tradition".

The château's history began way before the 19th century. It was owned by the Marquis de Mirabeau from the 16th to the 18th centuries – they were a political family who

enjoyed wine so much that one epicurean Marquis was nicknamed 'Mirabeau-Tonneau': the barrel.

Today, these pebbly soils are ideal for making Luberon wines. Thomas farms forty-two hectares of vines, keeping the yield low to improve quality and flavour. Clapier is between the vineyards of Provence and the Rhône valley: "the wines have the power of the Rhône and the sunshine of Provence, and at this altitude we get hard frosts, so the Burgundy grape pinot noir grows well and gives a touch of finesse."

Grapes are hand-picked for the top cuvée, only 2,000 bottles of which are made annually; the rest of the crop is harvested mechanically and Thomas believes this is the only way to take large quantities of grapes at optimal ripeness.

The little tasting room is next door to a 19th-century vat house (which still contains the original 240-hectolitre oak vats). A modern winery across the courtyard contains shiny stainless steel equivalents of these ancient 'foudres'. They make twelve wines here; a visit to the cellars is a must.

WINES

Château de Clapier, 'Soprano' Côtes de Luberon
Summer nights, freshened by mountain and river breezes, produce a fresh climate ideal for making great pink wine. Perfumed and pleasing, the red fruit aromas blend with a discrete whiff of vanilla that comes from nine months' ageing in large oak barrels. A perfect partner for East Asian or fusion cuisine, Thomas's Soprano is a serious rosé and a wonderful food wine.
Wines €6–€18

Thomas Montagne
Château de Clapier, 84120 Mirabeau
• Rooms: 4 doubles, €85.
  11 apts, €280–€1,491 per week.
• Meals: Restaurant 5km.
• Closed: Rarely.
• +33 (0)4 90 09 61 06 (B&B)
• +33 (0)4 90 77 01 03 (winery)
• www.relaisdugrandlogis.com (B&B)
• www.chateau-de-clapier.com (winery)

L'Abbaye de Saint Hilaire

VAR

A few miles east of Aix-en-Provence is a chain of limestone peaks dominated by the kilometre-high Mont Sainte Victoire. Paul Cézanne lived here in the 1880s and the mountain was a spiritual inspiration to him – just as it was to the medieval Christians who built the chapel at its summit. On the plains below is a wine estate named after the abbey buildings hidden within its pine-scented forests: the Abbaye de Saint Hilaire.

It's a huge estate of fifteen square kilometres of garrigue, forest and vineyards, but the welcome, from Sophie, her brother Philippe and their friendly team, is very personal. The family acquired the estate in the 1970s and set about diversifying the business. Sophie explains: "Wine is our main focus but there is so much for walkers, climbers and cyclists. There used to be a riding centre here and it was said that from the farm you could ride from sunrise to dusk without crossing a tarmac road!"

Furthest from the winery is an ancient farm, or bastide, called La Marotte where numerous apartments and small villas have been created within the old walls. Each has its own character but all share a traditional Provençal layout. Living areas face south with doors opening onto the courtyard; bedrooms have small windows set into the cooler north-facing walls. The original fabric of the building and its character remain. Stucco walls and ancient oak beams, arched oak doors and pitch pine floorboards give a rustic background to the furnishings – some antique, some contemporary. One or two of the gîtes have private patios; others share a big sunny courtyard. "For barbecues, everyone cooks together," says Sophie, "the ambience is always conviviale." Above the courtyard is a large pool edged by tree-shaded lawns.

Along a dusty lane are the giant vat houses and cellars and a very special auberge whose table d'hôtes menu includes home-grown produce. Where the track disappears into the

WINES

Domaine de L'Abbaye de Saint Hilaire, 'Cuvée Domeni' Coteaux Varois
An assemblage of regional red grape varieties, and a soupçon of the white grape rolle, produce an elegant bouquet of red fruit bursting with juice and an almost sweet finish. Saint Hilaire's chilled rosé wines are just the thing with grilled Mediterranean vegetables and a smoky shoulder of lamb cooked with bunches of wild rosemary. Try the sweet vin cuit (cooked wine) with a walnut gâteau.
Wines €5.10–€18

oaks and Aleppo pines you'll find the chapel that gave the estate its name. From here you can explore the maze of forest tracks on foot or in the saddle. In winter the horses roam free, grazing in the forest; this is a prime time to catch a glimpse of the hare, deer and boar.

"In winter too," says Sophie, "you see sheep grazing in the vines. It's an efficient solution: the sheep do our weeding between the rows so we don't need to use herbicides, and they leave a natural fertiliser!"

Natural viticulture, limestone and clay soils and the Mediterranean sun create the ideal conditions for the local grape varieties: ugni, clairette and rolle for the whites; grenache, syrah and cinsault for the rosés and reds. All are available in the little tasting room at the entrance to the domaine. Try the sweet estate-bottled liqueurs, spicy vins cuits ('cooked wines') and heady eau de vie. Provence is here, waiting to paint its colours onto the canvas of your memory, in olive groves and hilltop villages, lavender fields and charming vineyards.

Sophie Cossettini
L'Abbaye de Saint Hilaire,
Route de Rians, 83740 Ollières
• Rooms: 3 twins/doubles, €80.
  15 gîtes for 2-11,
  €266-€1,500, per week.
• Meals: Dinner €18-€25.
• Closed: January.
• +33 (0)4 98 05 40 10
• www.abbayesainthilaire.com

Domaine de Saint-Ferréol

VAR

In a remote landscape of forests, mountain streams and hilltop villages, Guillaume's ancestors built a farm. For three centuries the property was handed down from father to son; when the time came for Guillaume to take over, he and Armelle left teaching jobs and began a new life, in this quiet valley at the foot of the Bessillon hills. Since their arrival in 1979 they have restored the house, planted new vines and raised four children. Armelle taught German in Paris and informs guests about the wines of the Domaine in several European languages. "Meeting people from many different countries is one of the most rewarding aspects of our life here," she says.

A host of vines lay siege to the ancient bastide and clamour at its walls. Within the sanctuary of the shady quadrangle is a heavy oak door, behind which is a twisting stone staircase leading to the bedrooms. In keeping with the simplicity of the architecture, the three doubles and the suite are free of swags and bows; you find, instead, simple fabrics, plain walls and country furniture. Wide arched windows framed by cypress trees give onto pastoral views of the vineyards and, across the valley, you can see the towers of a crumbling château that rises above the village of Pontevès.

In the communal kitchen shared with the other guests there are a stone sink, a Provençal fireplace and modern appliances fitted discretely beneath a wooden countertop; if you love to cook, Armelle will advise on where to buy the best local produce. You can eat on the first floor or in the courtyard. There's a cottage, too, in the old wheat mill, with a private garden. Behind the house, in the cool shade of the pigeonnier, is a swimming pool surrounded by stone-terraced lawns.

Guillaume farms twenty-one hectares of vines on the south-facing slopes that rise from the valley to the tree-covered top of the hillside. Traditional methods of viticulture .

and winemaking are used to create a fresh citrusy chardonnay, a fruity rosé and a spicy red. "We began experimenting with carbonic maceration," says Guillaume, explaining how this modern trend involves the fermentation of whole red grapes in CO_2 gas to extract the fruity aromas and reduce the harsh tannins. "But rather than improving the fruit it killed it! So the following year we went back to the old ways." The red syrah and grenache blend is an unpretentious, square-shouldered red perfect for Provençal cuisine and is good value for money.

Ex-history teacher Guillaume is fascinated by Saint Ferréol's past. His collection of photographs taken at the turn of the last century show a corral of goats that gave the family meat and cheese, wheat being harvested in today's vineyards, and barrels of wine in the courtyard being loaded onto horse-drawn carts. Above the door to the winery is a sundial whose shadows have marked the passing days of many generations of this family. Families have come and gone but the house possesses a reassuring sense of timelessness

WINES

Domaine de Saint-Ferréol, Coteaux Varois en Provence
You can tell that a winemaker is proud of his wine when he puts his name on the label; Guillaume includes his address and phone number too. A blend of grenache and syrah produce a robust, rustic red with a pleasant red fruit aroma and a pinch of spice. It's an ideal wine to serve with hearty Provençal stews or with black olive tapenade spread on the famously tasty local bread, 'fougasse'.
Wines €4.60–€6

Guillaume & Armelle de Jerphanion
Domaine de Saint-Ferréol,
Domaine de Saint-Ferréol,
83670 Pontevès
- Rooms: 3 twins/doubles, 1 suite, €68–€75. 2 gîtes for 2-4, €380–€580 per week.
- Meals: Restaurant 2km.
- Closed: Rarely.
- +33 (0)4 94 77 10 42
- www.domaine-de-saint-ferreol.fr

Domaine des Aspras

VAR

Highland streams tumble through pine forests and craggy gorges. In the deciduous valleys they form lakes and rivers that carry the mountain waters over the plains and away to the sea. From the mountain tops, down through woods of beech and oak to the vineyards below, nature dresses the valleys in splendour. 'Green' Provence – la Provence Verte – is aptly named: not only for its natural beauty but for its many ecological projects in viticulture and tourism.

In the vanguard of the region's organic movement is France's first bio village, Correns, and a passionate organic winemaker called Michaël Latz. Michaël's parents were Jewish refugees who fled Nazi Germany in the 1930s to settle in Belgian-owned Burundi in Africa. In 1961, following the country's independence, they found themselves, once again, fleeing from turmoil and genocide. They moved to Correns and planted vines on the stony fields called Les Aspras (the Latin 'aspera' means jagged and also, poignantly, hardship or adversity). Thus was Domaine des Aspras born. Michaël and his wife Anne moved to Correns in 1978; Michaël was elected mayor in 1995 and set in place an ecological programme that involved the whole village.

In the middle of the sixteen-hectare vineyard is the Maison des Vignes. From the poolside balcony, gazing to distant hills, Michaël explains the move to organics. "In the 1990s, traditional wine production was running out of steam and the young people were having trouble finding work. It looked as though Correns might become a 'dormitory' town. Now that 95% of the land is organic, there are benefits to the village and its people. We have increased the value of our produce so school-leavers can follow in their fathers' or grandfathers' footsteps. Dairy products, vegetables and honey that carry the organic label have also created new opportunities." It's remarkable that a medieval village, a sustainable way of life

and a primordial wilderness have been successfully protected for the next generation.

Correns is a natural draw to visitors but the village is blissfully free of gift shops and estate agents. Over the ancient stone bridge across the river is the road to Michaël's vineyards and this wonderful gîte. Inside the bastide you'll find a great mix of understated style and cosy homeliness. Shelves packed with books line the walls of the huge living room; traditional furnishings and big sofas blend with fun 1970s chairs and abstract originals. The kitchen is a joy but you can also call upon a couple of Slow Food-inspired cooks from the village. Upstairs (on two floors) are six double bedrooms with hand-painted floor tiles and bold bathrooms. The ground-floor rooms open onto a broad terrace descending to a pool, a small garden and the vines.

Separate from the gîte is a little tasting room and boutique. Each of Michaël's wines carries the family motto, 'Connais-toi toi-même' ('Know thyself'). It speaks as much of the strong identity of the wines as that of their makers.

WINES

**Domaine des Aspras,
'Cuvée Reserve' Côtes de Provence**
Provence is best known for its rosés but the region gives us some excellent reds too. This Côtes de Provence is a rustic full-bodied wine with leather and liquorice mixed with rich black fruit. Firm, dry and long, it's simply delicious. Sommeliers often look to the northern Rhône valley for a wine to serve with venison or wild boar but Michael's Reserve goes perfectly with strong game dishes and rich sauces. Wines €4.50–€11

CUVÉE RÉSERVE 2006

DOMAINE DES ASPRAS

Côtes de Provence
APPELLATION CÔTES DE PROVENCE CONTRÔLÉE

Michaël Latz
Domaine des Aspras,
83570 Correns
- Rooms: 1 gîte for 12, €... per week.
- Meals: Restaurant 6km.
- Closed: Rarely.
- +33 (0)4 94 59 59 70
- www.aspras.com

Domaine de Garbelle

VAR

Leaving the village of Garéoult behind, the old road to Brignoles rises through fields of cereal crops and vines. Where the lane joins the ancient forest track are the Gambinis' olive groves and vineyards. In winter, after a double harvest (grapes in autumn, olives before the year's end) the vines are sleeping and all is peaceful. A ribbon of white smoke rises from the low-pitched roof of the house to a broad sky in cobalt blue. A well-fed donkey grazes between the vine rows, dogs bask in the early morning sun and there is a sense of contentment.

Mathieu Gambini came here from Corsica and married Michelle, a local girl. As the house was "just four walls and no roof", Mathieu undertook the complete restoration of the farm and vineyards. "We began by selling our grapes to the co-operative," he recalls, "but in 1988 we built the winery and since then we've been producing our own Coteaux Varois wines." Jean-Charles, their son, took over the

flourishing wine business when Mathieu and Michelle stepped back from day-to-day business. They now manage the chambres d'hôtes and organise two annual events: an antiques fair in August and a market garden jamboree in October.

The winery, inscribed on the outside with Louis Pasteur's famous line, 'Wine is the most healthy and hygienic of drinks', is a low, ochre coloured building containing a barrel cellar, vat room and tasting area. Next door is a conference room and, at the gable end, two guest bedrooms with glazed doors leading to the olive-scented courtyard. Inside the mood is cool and contemporary with light oak beams, terracotta floors and pale muted colours. Michelle serves breakfast at her farmhouse table and in the wintertime a fire of blazing vine roots fills the room with the evocative smell of wood smoke. The Gambinis are a charming couple who will reveal effusively the fascinating history of this place.

**Domaine de Garbelle,
Coteaux Varois en Provence Rosé**
Zesty fruit aromas come bounding out of the glass: pineapple, lemon, grapefruit and a hint of what the French call 'bonbons anglais' – sticky boiled sweets. This rosé is mouth-filling with a fruity finish. It is a wonderful partner to grilled red mullet served on a salad dressed with a red wine vinaigrette. Try the hearty red with a Corsican 'stufatu' meat sauce on fresh pasta.
Wines €6.50–€11.50

"Garbelle means 'wheatsheaf' in Provençal," Mathieu explains, "and the farm was producing wheat for bread, olives for oil and vines for wine well before the Revolution."

In the past, on farms like Garbelle, wine was made to be served to the family and to slake the thirst of the farm labourers. Much has changed over the past century and today Jean-Charles sells his wines all over France. "Our markets have changed," he says, pouring a splash of aromatic rosé into a tasting glass, "and so too have some of our methods, but we still harvest our red grapes by hand and the vines are still grown as naturally as possible." Jean-Charles's wines have a clean modern feel with bags of distinct, aromatic character. You must taste their delicious pale gold oil, too; olives are harvested at the end of November and taken to the seaside harbour town of La Londe to be cold pressed.

A trip to the Mediterranean is a short, dreamy journey over the foothills of the Massif des Maures and down to the coast where the herby smell of the garrigue is replaced by the fresh, salty aroma of the sea.

Mathieu Gambini
Domaine de Garbelle,
Vieux chemin de Brignoles,
83136 Garéoult
• Rooms: 2 twins/doubles, €65.
• Meals: Restaurant 1km.
• Closed: Rarely.
• +33 (0)6 08 63 91 00
• www.domainedegarbelle.com

Domaine du Fogolar

ALPES-MARITIMES

High in the hills above the suburbs of Nice, perched on a steep slope reached via vertiginous hairpin bends, is a fascinating winery. Jean Spizzo, originally from the Friuli in northern Italy, bought the house and planted the first vines here over thirty years ago. He named the domaine 'Fogolar', which means 'hearth and home' in his native Friulian. From the terrace the view is inspiring: vineyards descending to almond trees, with the Var valley and the rocky promontory of the Baou de Saint-Jeannet towering hundreds of metres above the river gorge.

"We wanted to make the most of the wonderful views, the light and the sun," says Jean, gazing at the distant mountains from the balcony of the gîte. "The living room opens onto south- and west-facing terraces and from the upstairs bedrooms you emerge onto an enclosed roof terrace." Furnishings are simple: kilim-covered terracotta floors, leather armchairs and country

furniture are functional rather than theatrical. It's easy to forget that you are only a few minutes' drive from the Riviera and the city of Nice – this is such a peaceful spot, disconnected from the noise and traffic just over the hill to the south.

Further up the slopes, a little way from the gîte, is the couple's family home, the winery and a small tasting salon. A hand-written sign welcoming potential buyers is typical of the Spizzo's understated but genuine charm. As diverse and vibrant as the colourful paintings that line the walls, Jean's rare Bellet wines are packed with aromas and flavour. White wine aficionados, rosé lovers and dyed-in-the-wool red wine drinkers will be delighted to discover these relatively unknown gems from France's most easterly vines.

The place name of the vineyards, located at the southern end of the Bellet appellation, gave Jean's wines the name 'Collet de Bovis'. Being close

to the wealth and celebrity of the Côte d'Azur, most of Bellet's produce is sold locally, but Jean has clients in the USA and the UK who adore these distinctive wines. What gives them such powerful aromatic qualities? "It's the natural factors that are most important," he says, unassumingly. "We have steep slopes of pebbly rock called 'poudingue' (from the English word 'pudding stone') and a mix of local grape varieties rarely found elsewhere." Thyme, grasses and wild flowers grow between the vine rows and insecticides are banned. The result of Jean's unique terroir (and his labours in the vineyards and the winery) is a wine that wins medals year after year.

The beaches and marinas of the Cote d'Azur entice those looking for glamour, but if you want to escape the crowds and the heat head for the hills. Grasse and its perfume houses are a short drive away and, beyond, are the mountains and lakes of the Var. Jean and wife Michèle organise exhibitions and performances so you could even come in the winter for warmth and art; the smell of almond blossom and citrus fruit warmed by the pale sun is a tonic in winter

WINES

**Domaine du Fogolar,
'Collet de Bovis Bellet'**
Grapefruit and lemon aromas leap out of the whites, such is the concentration provided by these high altitude, Côte d'Azur-ripened grapes. Superb with oysters, the mouthwatering juiciness of the wines goes equally well with fine fish dishes and rich sauces. Try the soft spicy red with roasts and stews, and the rosé, with its raspberry and iris undertones, as an aperitif.
Wines €14–€17

BELLET

Jean Spizzo
Domaine du Fogolar – Collet de Bovis, 370 chemin de Cremat, 06200 Nice
- Rooms: 1 gîte for 10, €800–€1,100 per week.
- Meals: Restaurant 4km.
- Closed: Never.
- +33 (0)4 93 37 82 52
- www.vin-de-bellet.com

WHAT IS SPECIAL?

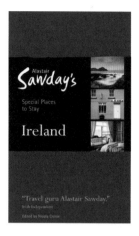

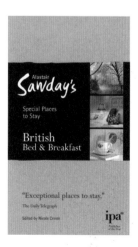

Alastair Sawday Publishing has created eighteen Special Places to Stay guides. Each one of our 5,000 properties has been visited, and chosen, by us because we like it, and its owners.

We take huge pleasure from finding people and places that do their own thing – brilliantly; places that are unusual and follow no trends, places of peace and beauty, and people who are kind and interesting – and who genuinely like meeting people.

Our books are founded upon a passion for the unpretentious, the authentic and the unique. Our criteria for deciding whether a place is special may appear obscure – we have no star system and do not include somewhere just because it has all the right 'facilities'. The things that count, for us, are people, architecture, history, views and, above all, atmosphere. A faded 17th-century palace run by a generous, spirited family would be chosen in preference over a slick, designer hotel with all the five-star trimmings but surly staff.

We like owners who know what they're doing but, perhaps more importantly, we like owners who enjoy what they're doing and who are generous with little things and generous in spirit. We like flexibility and a willingness to consider people's needs. We know that an encounter with genuine kindness and an easy welcome live longer in the memory than any number of 'facilities' that have earned gold or silver awards.

We are delighted that so many of our owners care deeply about good food. Much of what they serve – be it in a B&B, a hotel or an inn – is local, seasonal or organic. We ask all our owners about the food they serve and we highlight the efforts of those who try to avoid supermarket shopping for their breakfast ingredients and who source as much local and organic produce as possible. We give special coverage, too, to eco-friendly owners and have a book dedicated to eco-accommodation called Green Europe (see opposite).

So we have many more jewels in our crown, quite apart from the seventy-five or so special places in this book. You should look out, especially, for our other French guides (opposite) for they bring you a fascinating a collection of owners who run super B&Bs, Hotels and Châteaux, in the depths of the country, in towns and cities.

Use our website www.sawdays.co.uk to find out lots more about our Special Places worldwide. On the site you can find out exactly where each property is placed on our excellent maps, the make-up of rooms and bathrooms and which places best suit your needs when you are travelling with, say, children, pets or the less-mobile.

OUR OTHER FRENCH GUIDES

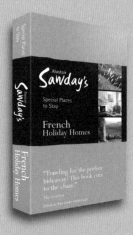

The Telegraph
"In the midst of a grey and gloomy British winter, Alastair Sawday's Gallic guide offers a cheering ray of sunshine. From the Loire to the Languedoc, Sawday unearths the most beguiling châteaux, auberges and hotels, all offering excellent food and liberal libations of wine."

Living etc
"Full of sumptuous châteaux, converted convents and rose-covered cottages. Spend a few hours with it and you won't be able to resist booking a holiday."

Everything France
"This is an indispensable guide that should not leave your side. Pray others don't find out about it, or the hidden gems it covers won't stay that way for long."

Sawday's guide to eco-holidays

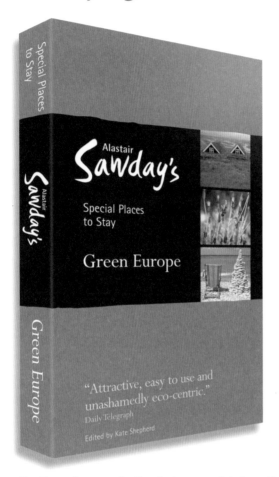

Our Green Europe collection features special places that go the extra mile to provide responsible holidays. You will find over 170 authentic, beautiful places to stay that champion organic food, use eco-friendly technologies, contribute to conservation, or have a positive impact on their community.

Choose from tree houses, yurts & tipis, country B&Bs, organic farmstays and eco-chic hotels. We've inspected and like them all. Countries covered include Britain, Ireland, France, Belgium, Spain, Greece, Portugal, Italy, Switzerland, Austria, Germany, Sweden, Norway, Denmark, Finland and Iceland.

Our fresh and lively write-ups paint an accurate picture of what to expect, from the welcome to the setting and there are clear maps, directions and symbols. Useful sections include a Green Glossary and information on travelling around Europe by train.

RRP £11.99; available for £7.79 + p&p on www.sawdays.co.uk/bookshop

SAWDAY'S FRAGILE EARTH SERIES

The Fragile Earth Series is a growing collection of campaigning books about the environment and an important part of our company. Highlighting the perilous state of our world yet offering imaginative and radical solutions and some intriguing facts, these books will make you weep and smile. They will keep you up to date and well armed for the battle with apathy.

For many years Sawday's has been 'greening' its business. Our aim is to reduce our environmental footprint as far as possible. (We once claimed to be the world's first carbon-neutral publishing company, but are now wary of such claims.) In recognition of our efforts, we won a Business Commitment to the Environment Award in 2005, and in 2006 a Queen's Award for Enterprise in the Sustainable Development category. In that year Alastair was voted ITN's 'Eco Hero'. In March 2008 we won the Independent Publishing Guild's Environmental Award.

The Big Earth Book
Updated paperback edition
£12.99

The Big Earth Book, by James Bruges, explores environmental, economic and social solutions for saving our planet. It helps us understand what is happening to the planet today, exposes the actions of corporations and the lack of government action, weighs up new technologies, and champions imaginative and viable solutions. Tackling a huge range of subjects, it has the potential to become the seminal reference book on the state of the planet – the one and only environmental book you need.

"A primer for all progressives, and a salutary lesson for the rest in what they missed by not taking the greenies seriously." *New Scientist*

"James Bruges deals effortlessly with topics from climate change to nanotechnology." *The Ecologist*

Money Matters
Putting the eco into economics
£6.99

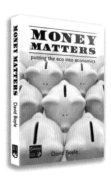

This well-timed book will make you look at everything from your bank statements to the coins in your pocket in a whole new way. It holds the potential to change your life. In a world where the richest man is able to amass a fortune of over $50 billion, but over half the population of the planet live on less than $2 a day, this book discloses alternative and fairer ways. In his pithy and well argued style, author David Boyle sheds new light on our money system and exposes the inequality, greed and instability of the economies that dominate the world's wealth.

Do Humans Dream of Electric Cars?
Your journey to sustainable travel
£4.99

It is estimated that there are over 600 million motor vehicles being driven on the streets of the earth. This figure is expected to double in the next 30 years. But oil is running out and bio-fuels are no longer seen as a viable alternative to fossil fuels.

This guide provides a no-nonsense approach to sustainable travel and outlines the simple steps needed to achieve a low carbon future. It highlights innovative and imaginative schemes that are already working, such as car clubs and bike sharing and is published to coincide with the Sustrans's Change Your World Campaign 2009.

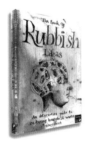

What About China?
Answers to this and other awkward questions about climate change
£6.99

A panel of experts gives clear, entertaining and informative answers arguing that the excuses we give to avoid reducing our carbon footprint and our personal impact on the earth are exactly that, excuses.

The Book of Rubbish Ideas
£6.99

Every householder should have a copy of this guide to reducing household waste and stopping wasteful behaviour. Containing step-by-step projects, the book takes a top-down guided tour through the average family home.

"Littered with good ideas about how to reuse and repair things rather than replacing them." *Healthy and Organic Living*

Also available in the Fragile Earth series:

Ban the Bag A community action plan	£4.99
One Planet Living A guide to enjoying life on our one planet	£6.99
The Little Food Book An explosive account of the food we eat today	£6.99

To order call 01275 395431 or visit our online bookshop
www.sawdays.co.uk/bookshop for up to 40% discount

WINE INDEX

• AOC (Appellation d'Origine Contrôlée)- A Government certification controlling the origin and production methods of French wines.

• VdP (Vin de Pays)- 'Country wines' that comply with regional rules governing the methods of production. Although mostly modest plonk, some VdP wines are superb.

TOWN INDEX